# MURDER IN LANCASHIRE

# MURDER IN LANCASHIRE

## Notorious cases and how they were solved

IAN HUNTER

Copyright © Ian Hunter, 2012

First edition, 2012

Published by Palatine Books,
an imprint of Carnegie Publishing Ltd
Carnegie House,
Chatsworth Road,
Lancaster, LA1 4SL
www.carnegiepublishing.com

The right to be identified as the authors of this work has been asserted by
Ian Hunter in accordance with the copyright, Designs and
Patents act 1988

*British Library Cataloguing-in-Publication data*
A catalogue record for this book is available from the British Library

ISBN 978-1-874181-91-0
Designed and typeset by Carnegie Book Production
Printed and bound in the UK by Page Bros Ltd, Norwich

# Contents

# Foreword

YOU MIGHT WELL THINK, WATCHING TV, that all crime is solved by a quick idea and swift action, all within sixty minutes to a fanfare of screaming tyres. It isn't like that.

Ian Hunter's account of some of the cases he has worked on during his career with the Lancashire Constabulary tells the truth; crimes are solved by careful observation and diligent inquiry, looking at what is there and, equally important, seeking what is not there.

This book tells the inside story of some of the most notorious cases over the past forty years or so. One or two took Ian Hunter and his colleagues far beyond the county boundaries – the Black Panther inquiry covered the Midlands and the North of England, while the Handless Corpse case had its origins in New Zealand. But all were solved with the essential qualities of every good detective – endless patience, relentless determination, and a sharp eye for even the smallest detail and unflinching courage. The moment when Ian Hunter and a colleague ran at the door with their shoulders, knowing that the double killer on the other side might still be holding a shotgun, is a chilling example of the kind of courage we expect of our police officers.

Ian Hunter never expected or intended to become a police officer. He had several jobs before he heard that the Lancashire Constabulary was looking for recruits in Scotland, where he was born and grew up. As a policeman he served in various parts of Lancashire and probably knows the county far better than those of us who have lived here all our lives.

He still has close links with Scotland, with both clan and community, but chose to spend his retirement in the county where, for so many years, he upheld the law with such distinction. Like all who know him, I'm glad he did.

Tom Sharratt

# Acknowledgements

**FIRST AND FOREMOST I SHOULD like to thank my wife Elsie for encouraging me to write this book, although we are both octogenarians who have celebrated our diamond wedding anniversary, and have reached the stage of extreme maturity.**

My thanks to my very talented grand-daughter Samantha Hunter, who at the age of sixteen years has typed every word of this book. Without her valuable assistance it would never have been written.

Thanks also for the help and guidance from a retired police colleague, Bob Dobson of Landy Publishing, for his advice regarding format and the benefit of his experience in book writing.

My gratitude to Sue Clarke for designing the layout of the book.

Lastly my thanks to Lancashire County Councillor Tom Sharratt, an immensely experienced retired journalist, for his advice and counsel, and for providing the foreword for this book.

# An Odd Ode

*Some time when you're feeling important,*
*Some time when your Ego's in bloom,*
*Some time when you take it for granted*
*You're the best qualified man in the Room,*
*Some time when you feel that your going*
*Would leave an infillable hole;*
*Just follow these simple instructions*
*And see how they humble your Soul.*

*Take a bucket and fill it with water,*
*Put your hands in it up to your wrists,*
*Pull them out and the hole that remains*
*Is the measure of how you'll be missed.*
*You may splash all you wish when you enter,*
*You can stir up the waters galore,*
*But Stop! and you'll find in a minute*
*That it looks just the same as before.*

*The moral of this is quite simple,*
*Do just the best that you can,*
*Be proud of yourself, but remember,*
*There is no indispensable Man.*

ONE

# Early Days

**I JOINED THE LANCASHIRE CONSTABULARY in 1956, served for thirty years and retired with the rank of chief superintendent in charge of Chorley division. Prior to that rank I was a detective superintendent, second in command of CID. I am now an octogenarian and having been retired for twenty-five years, with never a moment to spare, time has arrived for reflection.**

At the end of the war, aged fourteen years, I left school in Aberdeenshire, as many others did, with a very limited education, and without an academic certificate of any sort. On leaving school I served my apprenticeship as an electrician for five years, after which my services were terminated as was the custom in those years in order to employ another apprentice. I then sought work through any source available: farming, lorry driving, cutting wood; I spent time as an electrician and as a self-employed taxi driver. The thought never entered my mind that one day I might become a police officer.

In 1949 I was conscripted into a Highland regiment and trained at Fort George, Inverness, which involved ten weeks' initial and six weeks' advanced training; the latter for the Far East. After training I was retained on the staff with rank of lance corporal. The first contingent of recruits I was involved in training was posted to Korea during the outbreak of that war.

I decided that training was not for me and was detailed for an overseas posting to Egypt. We travelled by train through Holland to Austria, Italy to Trieste, then by boat

*1*

to Port Said. We stayed overnight in a transit camp in Austria, confined to camp with a free supply of cigarettes. Three of us, being non-smokers, decided to jump camp and have a look around. We soon found, as we did not have foreign currency, that in a suitable establishment two cigarettes could be bartered for one drink. It soon became apparent that many colleagues followed the same pursuit, and the military police arrived on the scene. We made a hasty retreat but, under the influence of alcohol, became separated from each other. I made my way to what I thought was the transit camp and into a Nissen-type hut and collapsed on a bed. I have no idea how long I lay there, but as daylight approached I was amazed at my surroundings. There were many beds, clothing, Wellington boots etc. and it was obvious that a great many people lived there. I was also amazed at the height of the fence I had climbed. I had no option but to climb it again. I formed the conclusion that the hut I had stayed in must have been some sort of displaced persons establishment. I eventually found the transit camp and crept in undetected. The following day on the way to Trieste, I saw my two colleagues in handcuffs being marched on to the troopship en route to Egypt.

The arrival at Port Said was the introduction to a strange new world; the weather was tremendous with clear blue skies and gentle blue waves. As our troopship docked we became aware of several young Egyptians swimming away from the dockside towards our ship. It soon became apparent that we were expected to throw coins into the water, which they dived for. Sometimes it took quite a while for the divers to reappear. Such was our introduction to a way of life in Egypt: begging or forever holding out hands for something for nothing. I was posted to a military malaria control post. In those days British troops were confined to the Suez Canal zone, and our camp was alongside the canal near to the town of Ismalia. Because our duties were the control of malaria we were supplied with civilian clothing in order to work

*The author whilst serving in Egypt — Malaria Control Unit, 1949–1950*

outside the restricted area. The strength of the unit was a captain, a sergeant and initially four men; again I was promoted lance corporal.

By the time I came to leave the unit I was working alone. We had four Egyptian drivers, two hundred male labourers, and an Egyptian chief clerk. Each morning I had to dispatch manpower into areas known for breeding mosquitos, such as areas of water swamps, but also local mud hut villages. Each squad of workers was controlled by a foreman called a 'rice'; they in turn were supervised by a leader called a 'bash rice'. These were very important employees and controlled manpower with the threat of a heavy stick. The work in this unit was of such a nature that I saw very little military activity. It meant an early morning start and an early afternoon finish when the heat became intensive. Our camp was situated near a lake which meant swimming every day.

I became very friendly with the Egyptian clerk and one day, in light of a domestic problem, he asked me to drive him to his home as quickly as possible. I agreed and on his instruction drove into Ismalia, where he lived, in an army jeep. I noticed we were entering a military restricted zone, but ignored the fact and carried on driving. Suddenly I found myself in a very unfamiliar scene. Streets littered with rubbish, loud music, stalls and traders standing practically shoulder to shoulder. Anxiously, I dropped the clerk off and followed his direction out of the area. As I approached a railway crossing the barrier dropped and I was brought to a halt. I stopped alongside a large group of women all dressed in black garb from head to toe and noticed a funeral procession walking toward us. A body was being carried in a wicker casket. As the procession got level to us the congregation of women started wailing. I realised at once that this was normal practice as described in the Bible – professional wailers at the scene of a funeral. I was astounded and so relieved when the railway barrier was raised that I went through the vehicle gears at speed to reach the camp again. I had a word with the clerk the following day to the effect – 'never again'. I enjoyed my period in Egypt and learned a lot about life in a different country. Army conscription in those days was eighteen months, but when on the troopship home for demob I was informed the term had now been increased to two years, so I had another six months to go. I was transferred into the Highland Light Infantry and served the rest of my time in the real army in Colchester.

In 1956 whilst self-employed as a taxi driver, a friend who was also struggling for work informed me that the Lancashire Constabulary was in Aberdeen on a recruitment drive. Quite a number of Lancashire police vehicles were parked outside Aberdeen city police headquarters, interviews were being conducted in caravans, and officers were giving out a large volume of information about the force. My friend was turned down because he did not measure up to the height standard. I was asked if I would undertake an entrance examination that night in the police headquarters. Fourteen of us sat the test and the papers were marked the same night, after which ten names were called out. My name was not amongst them. We were then told only the remaining four had passed. I was given a final interview and asked to visit Lancashire for a medical. I did so and three weeks later I was a police constable. At the time I was twenty-five, married with one of a family and living in a house in a quiet country area of Aberdeenshire.

The recruitment drive realised forty men from all over Scotland, and we all arrived at a police training centre at Warrington. Some were older than I was but nearly all were ex-service with much experience in life.

My first posting was to a mining area of Wigan, in lodgings awaiting a 'married vacancy' with accommodation for my wife and family who were still in Scotland. As constables we patrolled alone with no means of communication, but kept an hourly 'point' at pre-decided telephone kiosks. I very soon found out that my way of life was vastly different from that of some of those in the mining community. I received a call to visit an address where there had been a domestic dispute. On arrival I found a drunken miner whose wife lying bleeding on the floor of the house. She appeared to be badly hurt so I decided to arrest the miner. We had quite a struggle but I was fit and he was drunk. As I was removing the miner from the house his wife got up from the floor and attacked me. I very quickly got the message and left them to their own devices. She refused any medical help. I soon found out the miners work hard in terrible conditions and they also make the most of their leisure time in a manner that suits them.

I was only stationed at Wigan for a short while, then transferred to a married vacancy in Huyton, to the north of Liverpool. This meant moving household furniture from Aberdeenshire to Lancashire. Our furniture left on Sunday, and my wife, child and I travelled to Huyton on Monday.

5

When we arrived at the allocated house our furniture was not there, but arrived at ten-thirty that night. The whole police contingent on duty turned out to unload the vehicle. There were four police houses together and the wives came to our assistance. Later on, while discussing the move, one of the wives said she thought that when my wife and I spoke to each other we were speaking Gaelic.

Police foot patrol on Merseyside was similar to Wigan: no means of communication. And enlarged areas meant patrolling by cycle. The big difference was the vast amount of criminal activity. There was never a dull moment and I regarded it as a great police training area, providing considerable experience in arresting individuals for a variety of offences. Whilst patrolling it became apparent that many roads sparkled with broken glass and various roads had unaccountable areas of damage. I soon found out why, as on 5 November bonfires were lit in the middle of side roads. On discovering one such bonfire I was so incensed that I immediately dismantled it before it was lit. I was pelted with anything and everything, and a councillor who lived in the road opposite the bonfire came and thanked me, but he had done nothing himself. I carried on patrol, but on returning to the area the same bonfire was well alight.

On more than one occasion I arrested criminals in the act of committing an offence, resulting in a struggle and marching the offender in the dead of night to the nearest police station. On one such occasion I caught an offender actually breaking in to premises; his pockets were full of stolen property. At a subsequent court hearing the offender pleaded not guilty, and his defence solicitor accused me of beating his client and planting the stolen property on him. He was found guilty.

One night I was in bed when I heard a commotion outside. I got up, went outside and found a householder had caught an offender breaking into his house. I arrested the man and the following day I interviewed him at the police station. He informed me that he was an old lag with many convictions for crime. He said to me, 'You are a Scot. It is getting on to winter and I am bound to get a long prison sentence, at least I will be comfortable over the winter period with plenty of food. If you go to my house in Liverpool and get me my copy of Burns poetry I will confess all my outstanding offences.' I told him that I did not believe that a Liverpudlian like him could be a Burns follower. He, to my complete astonishment, started to recite Burns' poems in a realistic accent. He informed me he could stand any sentence as long as he had that book. Later I delivered his well-thumbed book and he admitted his outstanding offences – mainly burglaries.

After only four years as a foot patrol constable, I was invited to join the criminal investigation department. After serving in an area with a high crime rate I had gained much experience, leading to my first arrest for the crime of murder, that of Margaret Kerwin.

In 1963 after six years on Merseyside, I was transferred to Morecambe as a detective constable. In those days it was a very busy holiday resort exploited by criminals taking advantage of unsuspecting holidaymakers. My period there was short-lived, and in November 1964 I was promoted to uniform sergeant at Cleveleys, near Blackpool, a fairly quiet resort which gave me time to study. Whilst there, I passed two more examinations for further promotion. After two years I was moved back to Morecambe as a detective sergeant. My period there was even shorter than before and in May 1967 I was promoted back into uniform as an inspector in Lancaster.

In those days there was no Crown Prosecution Service, and police inspectors were responsible for presenting cases in magistrates' courts. It was only in serious cases such as murder that solicitors were employed to represent the police. In Lancaster there were several judicial areas using different courts. For example, the Lancaster Castle Assize Courts and the Shire Hall were used. Both courts were of tremendous historical interest and very impressive to enter and appreciate – the walls of the Shire

Hall are festooned with the coat of arms of centuries of Lancashire high sheriffs.

Being promoted to inspector I was aware of the responsibilities of prosecuting in court, but it is only when you achieve that rank that this becomes a reality. On my first week as an inspector, when I did not even have a uniform, the divisional chief inspector told me to be in his office on a Monday morning, which was a court day, and he would take me into court and introduce me to the bench of magistrates. I arrived in his office at the appointed time but he was not there. His office phone rang and I answered it. It was the chief inspector who explained that he was outside his house – the wind had blown his door closed and he could not get in to put on his uniform jacket. He said I would have to take the court. He told me that I would find a briefcase on his desk, and that 'it's the Assize Court – you have ten minutes to get there'. Speak of being thrown in at the deep end! I arrived at the court just as the magistrates took their places. I had not even opened the briefcase containing the court papers and I had no assistance to confirm that defendants, witnesses or police officers were present. Four solicitors sat there with knowing expressions on their faces as though they were aware of my predicament. I was half-way through the list when the chief inspector entered. He sat beside me for a short while then got up and said, 'I see you are doing alright,' and left me to it. I hasten to add that I got guilty verdicts against the clients defended by two of the solicitors present; such was my introduction to the rank of inspector. You can sink or swim.

I remained in the rank of uniformed police inspector for only three months when I was transferred to Accrington as detective inspector to take charge of the divisional CID. From there on my career changed dramatically. Gone were the days of routine police work; instead the world of criminality, with ultimate responsibility on a divisional basis for all crime committed in that area. I gained a great deal of experience in that capacity.

In 1969 the Lancashire Constabulary experienced tremendous turmoil owing to the amalgamation of several borough police forces, creating a massive police force of seven thousand officers. It was at this time that panda cars and task forces were created. It was during this period that I was selected to attend a six-month course at the police college at Bramshill, Hampshire, composed of three months' academic studies followed by three months' police studies. The course was of tremendous value, with students not only from the UK but also from abroad.

In July 1969 I was promoted to the rank of detective chief inspector, second in command of a task force in Blackburn. This is the best rank in the police force because responsibility can be passed up or down. It was during the next six years that I became deeply involved in major crime in Lancashire. In 1971 I was selected to attend an intermediate command course at Bramshill Police College, studying law and police work. In 1975 I was promoted to superintendent in charge of Blackburn sub division, which was in fact the previous Blackburn Borough police force with additional areas of Lancashire attached. My predecessor had been a member of the borough force since 1969 and had not yet adopted the Lancashire method of policing and administration. Many changes had to be made.

It was during my period at Blackburn that the National Front political organisation became prominent and the leader of the party, John Kingsley Read, had premises there. The ethnic minorities, mainly of Pakistani origin, had increased in population over the previous years and were now in a position to make their presence felt by submitting planning permission to convert buildings, or to construct mosques. This provoked immediate response from the National Front in that, in the first instance, low-level demonstrations were carried out in the areas where mosques were being considered. The scene changed fairly rapidly, with much more aggressive exchanges becoming evident. An example was when a

Pakistani bus driver was walking past a building site, the labourers employed there made derogatory remarks and one of them assaulted the driver. Shortly afterwards a considerable number of Pakistani people descended on the site and, in revenge, attacked the labourers with wooden weapons. There was a considerable disturbance and several injuries were inflicted, including one labourer who suffered a broken arm.

The activities of the National Front accelerated with more and more demonstrations through the centre of Blackburn. In all such occasions the demonstrations were infiltrated by a variety of organisations holding extreme political aims and views – exploiting and making a difficult situation worse. They were immediately identifiable through their tactics (uncommon even for the National Front) – the linking of arms and wearing similar apparel, including crash helmets.

These are only examples. On many occasions I had to attempt to contact leaders and discuss routes to traverse, and hopefully to agree on what was accepted and what was not. Vast police resources were necessary to protect members of the public and prevent damage to property. Some of these activists would co-operate to some extent. Others, including the National Front, would not. Fortunately during this very difficult period no lives were lost but many injuries were inflicted. The cost of policing such demonstrations was considerable. It took some time for peace to be restored, mainly owing to the leadership of the National Front moving away from Blackburn.

In 1976 I was transferred again as superintendent second in command of the territorial division of Chorley, and eighteen months later I was moved again as task force commander at Blackburn, with involvement in crime over a wide area including Preston, Leyland, Chorley, Burnley, Nelson and Colne. After only twelve months, in September 1979, I was promoted chief superintendent in charge of Chorley division and remained there for seven years until I retired in 1986.

*National Front demonstration, Blackburn, 1975–1976*

During my service in Chorley a great deal of my time was occupied investigating complaints against the police, but also demonstrations by the National Front seemed to follow me there. These activities were of much less significance than those in Blackburn and failed to continue. In 1981 tremendous disturbances, referred to as the 'Toxteth riots', broke out in Liverpool, which spread out to Manchester and, on more than one occasion, support groups to deal with these riots were provided by neighbouring forces including Lancashire. A second period of the Toxteth riots occurred in 1984.

On 8 July 1981 I was in charge of 140 men and deployed to Liverpool to back up the local force in dealing with the outbreaks of further disturbances. Things were fairly quiet that night up until around 11:00 p.m. when I received instructions to redeploy to Moss Side, Manchester. On arrival it was immediately apparent that things were vastly different to Liverpool. Riots had escalated to such a degree that the whole area was in complete chaos. Petrol bombs were flying in all directions, with a large contingent of demonstrators endeavouring to overpower the police.

With our reinforcement a stand was made with solid rows of police officers curtailing the advance of rioters. Petrol bombs rained on the police lines. Fortunately most fell short and exploded on the ground before us. It is hard to appreciate the scene unless you were there. The object seemed to be to harm or injure as many police officers as possible, or to destroy or damage property and deprive members of the community of their livelihoods.

As the demonstrations continued I was standing behind the main row of police officers when I saw a petrol bomb being thrown towards us. I could see that it would land about head height in the line of the policemen in front of me. I called out a warning and when the petrol bomb was about twelve feet away the flaming wick fell out and the bottle smashed onto a police officer's shield. Everyone in the vicinity was sprayed with petrol. It was a very busy night and the amount of damage to property was considerable, with shop premises broken in to and the contents looted. Fortunately none of the police officers involved that night was seriously injured. I was proud of the application to duty displayed by the police officers. Not a single complaint was made about this extraordinary police work which tested everyone significantly. Our tour of duty, which lasted for twenty hours, ended with a hearty breakfast being supplied by Manchester City police at 6:30 a.m.

In 1985 I was appointed by the chief constables of Lancashire and Merseyside, with the approval of the chairman of the complaints against police authority in London, to carry out extensive enquiries in Merseyside regarding complaints against the police which arose from riots and serious public disorder in Liverpool in 1984. With a team of Lancashire detectives, and under the supervision of a retired sea captain appointed as an independent observer, I completed the inquiry and presented my findings to the Home Office in London. No further action was taken against any police officers. In the course of that inquiry I had the pleasure of interviewing the two main religious leaders of the city, the Reverend

David Shepherd and the Very Reverend Dr Warlock, who were both witnesses to the riots.

I retired in 1986 after thirty years of service, during which I was twice commended for 'keen work and initiative'. After twenty-two years I received the Police Long Service and Good Conduct medal provided by the police authority. On retirement I was presented with a certificate signed by Chief Constable Brian Johnson which described my conduct as 'exemplary'.

Reflection has influenced me to write about some of the important cases in which I was involved, and I want to tell the reader something about them in the following pages. But first, I will try to get over to the reader something of the disciplined organisation involved in the modern investigation of murder cases.

*Chief Superintendent Hunter receiving the 22 years police medal from the Chief Constable Brian Johnson, 1978*

# TWO

# Murder Investigation

MURDERS ARE USUALLY COMMITTED AS a result of domestic issues, love affairs, family disputes and grievances, where parties involved know each other. They are referred to in CID circles as 'one and one' – i.e. one committed, one detected. They involve very few enquiries but a vast amount of paperwork.

The alternative is a murder committed when the assailant is unknown and the scene indicates an unlikely association between the killer and the victim. Whether inside or outdoors, protection of the scene is paramount. Much valuable evidence can be destroyed through lack of thought by the first person at the scene, such as wiping away valuable fingerprints or blood stains, or treading on foot impressions left by the assailant. Footprints can be as valuable as fingerprints. No two shoes can display the same marks or striations, or damage to the soles, provided the impressions can be lifted or photographed. The most difficult scene to be protected is when a victim, though badly injured and likely to die but still alive, has to be removed to hospital. The preservation of life is obviously more important than anything else. Great care should be made by police officers at the scene to record everything done and include a comprehensive note of all persons at the location, along with a log of everything removed or left at the scene. In the event of the victim dying, the locus becomes so important when extensive searches and examination of articles or materials are conducted.

If life is extinct then specialists must be summoned to the scene. A doctor to confirm death, a senior detective, a Home Office pathologist, forensic scientists, photographers, fingerprint experts, a plan drawer, and other specialists, depending on the circumstances. All these individuals should be present before the body is moved and the facts logged.

No two murders are identical. The senior detective present will assess the situation in order to determine the extent of the necessary investigation after a post mortem has confirmed the cause of death. Whilst the initial action is taking place, that officer will have communicated with his headquarters to arrange suitable accommodation and manpower as near as possible to the scene of the crime. Sometimes the nearest police stations are unsuitable and alternative buildings can be acquired for the purpose. The ideal premises should have several rooms, toilet facilities, a limited kitchen and a large hall to accommodate a large consignment of detectives. Several telephones will be installed and computer lines arranged, and the necessary furniture to accommodate a pool of typists. Hopefully briefing of personnel will take place at 9:00 a.m. the next day, followed later the same day by a press/media conference. These premises will now be referred to as 'murder control'. It is the nerve centre of the operation and inside the manpower is controlled (this involves a daily debriefing) and responsibilities allocated.

The method of deploying manpower in the Lancashire Constabulary is by the use of a well-tried system which has been modified and improved over the years with the introduction of computers. It is not claimed that its implementation will always result in a satisfactory conclusion, but it is designed to ensure that the chances of evasion are minimal. It is also of prime importance that detectives attend both junior and senior CID training courses.

It is first necessary to arrange an experienced indexing team with computer facilities. Every statement or document must be perused with every item of interest properly recorded. No information by word of mouth should be accepted but that it is also recorded on paper.

A staff officer will be appointed to ensure that the senior detective officer's instructions are implemented, and to facilitate the general function of the control room. An exhibits officer will be responsible for the collation, recording and safe custody of all exhibits.

A detective chief inspector will be appointed to lead a number of squads such as:

- Background squad to research the victim

- Follow-up squad to follow up all generated enquiries

- Re-interview squad

- *Modus operandi* squad to investigate offences of a similar nature

- House to house enquiries squad

- Any other squad depending on the nature of information which comes to light, for example if taxi drivers are involved

A trust must be developed between the press/media and the detective in charge. There is nothing worse than the media making assumptions or developing unfounded suspicions. Proper questions are put with accurate answers. Press reporters can be of immense value and often provide valuable information. The days have gone when the attitude was 'tell them nothing'. Several golden rules apply to murder investigations:

- Proper elimination of the person who finds the body or reports the crime, and likewise the person who last saw the deceased alive

- Take nothing for granted, and believe nothing unless the facts can be proven

- Commit everything to paper
- Everything should be done to encourage and stimulate members of the squads to highlight information or suspicions

Murder investigations are geared to detecting the assailant(s); long hours are worked. Every man and woman needs to work to their best. No short cuts are acceptable in the search for a true result. Experienced detectives know, through mainly developed instincts, when the right questions are put and true answers are received when interviewing suspects.

In every murder case the senior detective will note any significant method or weapon used in the course of committing the crime. He will only share that aspect with his staff officers, so that when interviewing a suspect, matters may come to light known only to the detective and the suspect.

The ultimate responsibility for all policing matters rests with the chief constable. All aspects of crime investigation are delegated to the head of CID, usually a detective chief superintendent. That position is usually occupied by a detective of immense experience, a person of tremendous personality, well respected and capable of carrying out their responsibilities with enthusiasm and demeanour. It is obvious that the decision to appoint a detective to that rank must be carefully considered.

Throughout the country success is usually experienced in detecting murders, but periodically extremely difficult cases arise, sometimes covering wide geographical areas, and several different police forces. Occasionally conflicts of interest or the following of false leads can cause problems. Two cases which highlight the difficulties are the Yorkshire Ripper, a renowned multi-killer of females over a period of years, and the kidnap and murder of Lesley Whittle by the Black Panther in West Mercia, a serial killer discussed in a following chapter. In both cases, after many months of dedicated investigation, the offenders remained at large. It was apparent that the chief constables lacked confidence in the heads of CID. They were not satisfied with the lack of success in detecting the murderers or the apparent conflicts between the two police forces. Ignoring the reasons why they had been appointed in the first place, the lead detectives were transferred to other duties. A replacement obviously found himself in a difficult position, appraising the vast amount of paper work accumulated by a large squad of detectives. In both cases surely the problems could have been resolved in a different manner. Fortunately, these are infrequent occasions. The removal and replacement of the leader of the inquiry has an adverse effect on the murder squads, who, in prolonged inquiries, become a tightly knit team.

*The Squirrel Tie – the 'badge' for CID courses. A different necktie was designed for many murder inquiries*

It is hoped, with the more sophisticated technical and scientific equipment available today, that difficult murder inquiries will become slightly easier to handle.

The two most important attributes for a detective to have are training and experience. The Lancashire Constabulary Training School caters for the former, and arranges both junior and senior criminal investigating courses, which are sponsored by the Home Office, and open to pupils from all over the UK. These courses are usually for an extended period with examinations at the end.

Visiting lecturers attend these courses which, in the past, included a Preston solicitor, James Wilde. He was extremely small in stature but massive in demeanour and ability. He used to indicate that dealing with legal complexities was similar to detectives investigating cases, in which it was essential to keep your eye on the ball. He compared it with walking through a wood chasing a squirrel, the object being to catch the squirrel and not be distracted by all the other objects such as the trees, bushes, and other objects of less importance set to confuse the issue. The lesson was considered to be of such importance that a squirrel necktie was designed, depicting a red squirrel with different backgrounds, to be worn by members attending the course.

The later part of the course includes an exercise to investigate a murder. A scene will be set of a murder indoors where a volunteer acts as a victim. Various clues are displayed, some obvious and some partly obscured, such as fingerprints, fibre, blood stains etc. A lecture is delivered by a senior detective on the art of examination and protection of the murder scene. Everything seen and done will be recorded by an experienced detective, nominated as the staff officer to the senior detective leading to the inquiry. Other specialists attending the lecture will submit reports on their findings on examining the scene. The object is to make the exercise as realistic as possible.

Members of the course will be divided up into groups and provided with a script of the exercise, including details of witnesses to be interviewed and the general circumstances of the case. The initiative now rests with each group to appoint a leader and decide on how to proceed with the murder investigation. Which witness to interview? Who will be located either inside or outside the premises following their normal way of life or employment? It is important that these witnesses are played by experienced detectives who are following detailed scripts. These scripts indicate that if students ask the right questions, they should receive positive answers. If, on the other hand, they ask the wrong questions, the responses will be at the discretion of the witnesses who may lay out any sort of goose chase they choose. If the right questions are asked the inquiry will proceed on to the next witness, including studying the other experts' reports.

The exercise goes on for several days, culminating in the arrest of the suspect. The latter part of the exercise is always the most interesting. Some arrests are conducted by good police work; some suspects react violently on being arrested and put the teams to the test. Bearing in mind that the students are usually young and the witnesses not so young, a good old individual will not beat a good young detective. On one occasion the investigating team failed to arrest their suspect and he made good his escape. When the team realized their mistake they went looking for him and found him in the middle of a duck pond – up to his knees in water and mud. He had prepared to be in suitable clothing. He called to the team, 'if you want me come and get me!' or words to that effect. The arresting team had no option but to comply and arrest the suspect who did not come quietly. The arresting team were not suitably dressed and required the service of a laundry afterwards. The lesson learned in this case was to 'follow the squirrel' and not be distracted by any attempt to obstruct your objective.

Some of the students may have been involved in murder inquiries in their own forces before the course, but others may not. In an assessment of the exercise afterwards the students usually express their satisfaction in arresting the suspects and the value brought home to them of the many problems that can be encountered in a murder investigation.

In murder investigations it is essential that experienced detectives form the main bulk of the inquiry teams. Every one of them will have commenced his or her police career as a constable. Over time it will become obvious that some have a distinct leaning towards criminal investigation work and should be considered for that department after due assessment and interviews.

On being appointed a detective from a police constable, the most dramatic change from routine report writing was the preparation of paperwork for court files. Routine police work usually meant writing a brief outline of an incident, a traffic offence or other misdemeanour committed in the course of daily activities. As a constable the introduction to report writing was in using an old cast iron typewriter, usually with one finger. Very few police officers had ever used a typewriter before joining the police service.

In CID paperwork for court files becomes part of the daily routine, but it is time consuming in some serious or complicated crime investigations. Typists are available but are usually fully committed in preparing work of a more serious nature for senior detectives. There was no option but to use the old dilapidated typewriter readily available in each office.

Time and commitment leads to expertise, and undertaking work into serious crime ultimately leads to murder investigations.

Press reports relating to murder investigations often refer to the horrifying circumstances where 'even experienced detectives were sickened by the injuries inflicted'. I have never known a case where this expression applies. For the following reasons every police constable, at a very early stage in his career, will become involved in the syndrome of sudden death. Bodies are found in many

*Lancashire Constabulary Training School – senior detective course, murder exercise. Detectives come from all over the UK. Lecture by Detective Superintendent Hunter.*

different circumstances without suspicious circumstances. A constable will be allocated to deal with the case and follow the correct procedure, that is inform the local coroner, remove the body to a mortuary, track relatives to identify the corpse, attend the necessary post mortem and submit a report. This procedure will apply many times during his career, leading to familiarity with what appears to be an onerous task. The extremity of this task is experienced when dealing with suicide involving a train.

Even when dealing with sudden death, there is always room for humour. One day I entered a police station and found a sergeant and a constable taking off their uniforms. I enquired why and was told about an unusual set of circumstances. A report had been received from a member of the public that an elderly neighbour had not been seen for some time and fears were expressed for her safety. The officers went to the scene and found that several bottles of milk were on the doorstep, newspapers were protruding from the letter box and the curtains were drawn. There was no response to door knocking so a decision was made to force an entry. The house was cold and in darkness. On moving upstairs they saw the elderly female occupant, deathly white, lying in bed. The sergeant looked at his watch and declared that it was half an hour before the end of his shift, and that if they moved quickly they could conclude the removal of the body to the mortuary. The sergeant pulled back the bed clothes and, as he did so, the female occupant immediately yelled out, reached under the bed, grabbed a chamber pot and sprayed the contents over the two police officers. The situation created much comment from their colleagues.

A very serious aspect of murder investigation is to appreciate the devastating effect experienced by parents or family when a sibling or close relative goes missing from home, or is brutally murdered. There are many examples of this throughout the country, as far back as the Moors Murders committed by Brady and Hindley, and the more recent murder of Jo Yeates in Bristol at Christmas 2011. It is essential to appoint a liaison officer to maintain contact with the relatives and keep them informed regarding the investigation. It is impossible to describe the full extent of the grief felt by family members, something that will always be with them.

On one murder investigation I was involved in, a thoroughly experienced detective sergeant was appointed as a liaison officer to a local church frequented by a murder victim. That sergeant was dedicated to his work, and I was fully aware that it was impossible to overload him with murder inquiries. He took everything in his stride and never once complained. That particular murder investigation was prolonged, but subsequently concluded with the arrest of an offender. To my complete amazement I discovered that the sergeant had become a religious convert to that particular faith. He was no longer capable of following his career as a detective and left the police force to become a preacher. In due course I was informed that he went on a religious mission to America and met his very sad death in a plane crash.

The other murders which I have enumerated in this book are but samples of many more that are experienced in the course of a detective's service. No two cases are similar, and in each and every one, new experiences and lessons are learned. Some refer to CID work as a career, not because of the long hours worked, the sometimes extended miles to travel to and from crime scenes daily, the dedication to determine a positive results in every case, but because it becomes a way of life. When an inquiry reaches a crucial stage it cannot be left until a following tour of duty to be continued, important information must be completed immediately. When a murder has been committed, irrespective of the time of day or night, senior detectives are informed to attend immediately. It is just too bad if you happen to be sitting down to your Christmas dinner when the call is received. The Christmas period is often referred to as the 'silly season', when excessive drinking during the holiday period seems to trigger violence and even worse. Many other specialists, such as forensic scientists and pathologists, find themselves in a mortuary at 3:00 a.m. wishing each other a merry Christmas or happy New Year. I have found that pathologists are an incredible band of professionals, no matter what situation you are in they never fail to explain some aspect of the human anatomy which raises interest during a post mortem. Once a cause of death has been established and the briefing of detectives has taken place an incredible air of anticipation becomes apparent, and once areas of responsibilities are allocated there is an obvious anxiety to get on with designated enquiries. Exactly the same situation is apparent during press conferences, with the main difference being the abundance of questions asked.

THREE

# Task Forces

IN 1969, THE LANCASHIRE CONSTABULARY amalgamated with several independent borough police forces within the county. A period of considerable upheaval was experienced which raised the strength of the force from over 3,000 to over 7,000. Many of the borough chief constables became assistant chief constables. Reorganisation resulted in the county being divided up into five regions, each with an assistant chief constable in command. It was also decided to establish task forces in each region to deal with extraordinary public disorder, major crime situations and to support divisions with any developing day to day policing problems.

Each task force was commanded by a detective superintendent. Their strength also included a detective chief inspector, an inspector, several sergeants (both CID and uniformed crime patrol), uniformed mobile constables, dog handlers and drug squads. Problems were researched daily and deployments arranged whenever the need arose, for example football matches, outbreaks of hooliganism, general disorder or crime. Some of the personnel were authorised firearm officers. These task forces were available for immediate movement into any area of Lancashire.

As a detective chief inspector I was a member of No. 2 district task force, commanded by Detective Superintendent Wilf Brooks. The area we covered included Blackburn, Preston, Chorley, Leyland, Nelson and Colne, but depending on the necessity, several task forces could be used together to deal with major events, such as during the period when the Springbok Rugby South Africa team toured the UK resulting in massive demonstrations wherever they played rugby. Similar movements of police strength were necessary when dealing with National Front activities. More impact policing was arranged in No. 2 district region mainly owing to outbreaks of crime or public disorder. Every such deployment was as a result of daily or weekly research into current trends in crime etc. Briefings were held at various locations and precise details of the problems explained to the various patrols. There is no doubt that this type of policing proved hugely effective. Speedy mobility was a factor, particularly of the uniformed officers whose work as crime patrols was portrayed on national television as 'Z Cars' and 'Task Force', which has been described as 'a tool in the hands of a detective superintendent'.

The CID side of task forces concentrated on crime and criminals. The vehicles were fully equipped with the necessary stationery and materials to deal with major inquiries, such as murder or similar serious crime. In the event of a major crime they were invariably the first to arrive at the location. They were fully experienced in setting up murder controls and in the organisation of investigations which accumulated vast amounts of paperwork. Various squads are established as explained in the murder investigation chapter of this book, but it takes experienced leadership of the various squads to ensure that inquiries are conducted satisfactorily. Every statement obtained is circulated to each squad leader so that they are aware of the progress of the inquiry. Training and experience are both needed and squad leaders will have a junior detective at their side learning the procedure. CID strength to task forces was by careful selection from routine divisional personnel who have proven ability in crime detection.

In 1974 the Lancashire Constabulary was restructured and large areas were transferred to Greater Manchester and Merseyside. More upheaval and a much smaller Lancashire Constabulary meant a lot of task forces became unfashionable and much reduced in size and function.

It was during this period of service in task forces that I gained a vast amount of experience in major crime which resulted in becoming a visiting lecturer to the force training school. I covered such matters as current trends in crime and ultimately in murder investigation.

# FOUR

# Murder of Margaret Kerwin
## Huyton, 26 April 1963

**THIS WAS THE MURDER** of a 33-year-old by an
ardent admirer who had been a previous boyfriend.
The killer was so incensed by her recent marriage
that if he could not have her as a wife, then no one
could.

Less than a month after her marriage, Margaret
Kerwin was walking with her mother in a street in
Huyton, when they were attacked by 27-year-old William
Edward Spendlove, a labourer. He was armed with a
knife and rained blows on his unfortunate victim, who fell
dying in the road. It transpired that two years previously
Spendlove had lived only a few doors away from Kerwin,
who was then single, and he became infatuated with
the deceased, but she ignored or rejected his advances.
Spendlove moved away to another part of the town which,
according to relatives, was an attempt to forget about
the matter. Nothing much transpired until about a week
before the murder when Spendlove learned that Kerwin
was married and was believed to be pregnant. According
to relatives, the news upset him quite considerably and he
brooded over it for several days. On 20 April he appeared
to have got over it and left his home in quite good spirits,
but about 3:30 p.m. the same day he stabbed Kerwin to
death. His sister explained that he was passionately fond

of Margaret Kerwin, and that she was the only girl that he had ever taken an interest in. As Spendlove made his escape, a passerby made an attempt to stop him, only to be threatened with the knife which was still in his possession at that time. Spendlove made good his escape. A murder control was set up at Huyton Police Station and extensive searches commenced.

On 26 April I was absent from Huyton giving evidence in an assault case at Liverpool Assize Court. I returned to the police station completely unaware that a murder had been committed. The divisional head of CID, Joe Hampton, informed me of the facts, gave me the offender's name and a brief description. Everyone in the section was deployed. I was allocated a police car with another detective constable. As I left, Joe's instructions were ringing in my ear: 'use your initiative and make some enquiries.' In other words look as if you are busy.

Huyton is situated on the outskirts of Liverpool and I immediately put myself in his position – what would

*Margaret Kerwin, murdered by William Spendlove, Huyton, Merseyside, 1963*

he do? The brief information I had was that this was a crime of passion where the parties knew each other. The obvious means of escape from the area would be by bus, taxi, or being Liverpool, by boat. My first port of call was to visit the famous Lime Street railway station; this is a large station and took some time to search with a negative result. The next scene to search was the pier head. Ferries left there continuously to various areas on the other side of the Mersey.

About 6:45 p.m. the same day I saw a man in an obviously distressed state. He was pale and seemed by the state of his clothing to be unaware of the cold weather. I asked if his name was Spendlove and he replied, 'No, it's Edwards, I live across the water. I am waiting for a ferry.' His jacket being partly open I saw blood staining on his shirt. I opened his jacket and saw a blood-stained knife sticking out of his inside pocket. I realized immediately that he was the killer. He admitted his identity and explained that he would never get peace now. He also explained that his feeling for Kerwin had gone on for seven years. He said that he would have married her. 'If they hang me, or if they don't, I will commit suicide.' There is little doubt that if he had not been arrested he would have caught a ferry, only to jump overboard. Spendlove duly appeared at Liverpool Assize Court and was sentenced to life imprisonment. My first arrest for murder, when realizing what he had done, made the hairs on the back of my neck rise.

Many years afterwards I was working in Preston on a serious offence. I was examining the photographs of prisoners on day release from Preston prison who were suspect for the offence. The first picture I examined was Spendlove. He was near to the stage of being released from prison.

FIVE

# Double murder at Pudsey, Yorkshire

## 15 February 1970

A PERFECT EXAMPLE of a No. 2 district task force deployment was when a double murder was committed at Pudsey, West Yorkshire, on 15 February 1970. Help was sought from the neighbouring force of Lancashire.

Just after midnight on Sunday 15 February an automatic alarm rang at Pudsey Police Station, arousing an immediate response by several police officers to Sunny Bank Mill. The building was equipped with silent invisible ray alarms, meaning that intruders might still be inside the premises. The installation of this sophisticated equipment suggested that the premises had been frequently attacked and it was hoped that these offenders would be arrested. It was also known that a night watchman patrolled the interior of the premises and he may have activated the alarm. Nevertheless urgent police action was necessary and on arrival at the premises they hammered on an exterior door with no response. A police inspector arrived at the scene and he decided to climb over the main gates into the premises. He must have concluded that all was not well, or perhaps it was a false alarm, but he had to make sure. He instructed a constable to try and contact the night watchman by phone. The key holder, a works engineer with a house inside the mill premises, was alerted and set out across the mill yard with his dog. He saw the police inspector, who had apparently heard a noise, and found himself facing a crouching figure holding a shot gun. The inspector was heard to order the intruder to put the gun down and give himself up. The intruder then discharged the shotgun at close range, fatally wounding the police inspector. The key holder, accompanied by a police constable, reached the inspector and immediately attempted to summon an ambulance using the constable's radio. Not sure that the message had got through they decided to use the phone in the night watchman's office. On entering that room they found the watchman lying dead in a pool of blood. It transpired that he had been shot twice, once in the body and secondly in the head. He had not been murdered but executed, giving a very pertinent view of the demeanour of the criminal.

In the meantime tremendous police resources had been activated. A constable saw a suspect jumping over a wall of the premises and gave chase but could not get close to him, however at least this indicated his escape route. At 5:00 a.m. several police officers were in a police car on the outskirts of Pudsey when they saw a suspect climbing a wall off the road way into a field. On peering over the wall they saw a man holding a shot gun. They called to the suspect, identifying themselves as police officers and to give himself up, but his response was to continue with his escape and he discharged the shot gun again in their direction. The area was surrounded by police cars, their headlights trained on the fields. Even emergency generators were brought to illuminate the scene. By the time daylight came the whole district was swarming with police officers, some armed, and dog handlers, supported by helicopters carrying armed police officers. However the double killer had made good his escape. An investigating team collected evidence including the interviewing of police officers who had glimpsed the killer. They perused photographs of suspects. It was realised that the killer was Neil George Adamson, a 31-year-old local criminal referred to as 'the mad dog of Pudsey'. He had previously been convicted of stabbing one of the police constables involved in the search and had been sentenced to three years in prison for that wounding offence. The double murder and subsequent discharge of the shot gun at the police indicated that he was living up to his reputation as a mad dog.

Extensive though the searches were, the assailant had made good his escape. Enquiries were made of Adamson's relatives and associates. A member of the criminal fraternity, who must have been very close to Adamson, informed the police that he had gone to Colne in Lancashire. That information was passed to Lancashire Constabulary headquarters. At that time I was a detective chief inspector in No. 2 district task force station in Blackburn.

At 11:45 p.m. on Monday 16 February 1970 I was told that Adamson was suspected to be in Colne, Lancashire. With the task force commander we arranged a full deployment into the area. We were fully aware of the double murder in Pudsey. Knowing the seriousness of the situation we also obtained emergency lighting, a public address system, armed police officers, dog handlers and crime patrols. A taxi driver was quickly located who informed us that he had taken a suspicious, rough looking individual to an address in Colne. That house was quickly surrounded, a light was burning in the lounge but the curtains were drawn closed. Enquiries revealed that the suspect, Adamson, was there. The public address system was used to inform the occupants of the house that the police had surrounded the area and that we knew the culprit was in there. In view of Adamson's conduct in Pudsey with a shotgun, and his lack of response in Colne, a stand-off situation developed.

Detective Matthews and I approached the front of the house, and on standing on a small wall at the front of the premises we were able to look through a small window above the door. We saw a man of Adamson's description lying on a chair covered with a travel rug.

It was obvious that he must have been aware of the police activity outside, but he refused to surrender. The detective constable and I had a brief discussion on a course of action. We stood back and together lunged at the door which burst open. We were immediately followed by the head of Lancashire CID, Joe Mounsey, who had just arrived at the scene. Adamson did not even have time to make a move before he was arrested. He was taken to Colne Police Station to await the arrival of the West Yorkshire police. Fortunately at the time of his arrest Adamson did not have his shotgun.

I arrived home at 8:00 a.m. to have a quick shave, take some breakfast and then travel to Lancaster Assizes to give evidence in a robbery case. Such was life in a task force.

Adamson duly appeared at Crown Court where he pleaded guilty to the murder charges and was sentenced to life imprisonment with a recommendation that he serve at least thirty years in jail.

A newspaper cutting from 'The Weekend', June 1973, reporting on the outcome of Adamson's trial.

Neil Adamson . . . a violent thug who was jailed for life

Barry Taylor . . . He led police team

A VIOLENT thug who thought nothing of murder started a life sentence last night.

He left the court with a judge's recommendation of 30 years in prison still ringing in his ears.

Double murderer Neil Adamson was unmoved as he heard sentence passed . . . just as he was when he talked in prison of why he shot a night watchman for a second time because he was still alive.

He told police then : "I figured I would get no more for murder than for attempted murder and you know dead witnesses cannot talk."

Mr. Justice Cantley's words at Leeds Assizes wrote the final chapter in 31-year-old Adamson's story of five days of violence which ended with a four police force manhunt.

After recommending that the life sentence should be a minimum of 30 years, Mr. Justice Cantley told Adamson: "I don't mean by that to give you any reason to hope that after 30 years you will be released."

Adamson, a labourer, of Primrose Hill, Pudsey, had pleaded guilty to the murders of night-watchman Ian [...] woman partially blind and with a walking stick asked Adamson and a friend if they would help her home through the fog. They guided her to some waste ground where they attacked her.

years in jail for at the neck.

Even in the bar life of prison he During one of his finement in Armle he smashed a [...]

# SIX

# Some cases involving children

REPORTS OF CHILDREN MISSING FROM home can be very difficult to investigate if the initial information received is not handled properly. Many reports of missing juveniles received by the police are resolved in a short period of time to the satisfaction of all concerned. Occasionally, cases are recorded with an entirely different dimension.

Assessment of the circumstances is the most important consideration in every case. In some cases the information is received by civilian members of police staff and it is imperative that they are fully conscious of the need to alert supervisory police officers, so that a constable is dispatched to investigate. He must interview the informant be it a wife, mother, husband or guardian, to form an impression of the individual and the home circumstances. Children of a tender age sometimes innocently wander away with friends or, at the other extreme, are snatched away, assaulted and even murdered by offenders of unnatural paedophile sexual tendencies. I will give examples of serious crimes committed against children later in this chapter to illustrate the need to repeat careful assessment of every case.

The inquiry must determine if there is a possible reason for the absence of the child. Are there family problems? Was the child chastised at home or at school? Has he or she been missing before, if so under what circumstances? The time factor is most important. Was it during the day or had the missing child failed to return from school or been sent shopping in the vicinity? Cases have been experienced where children have crawled into disused garden furniture or cupboards or other likely places and have been unable to free themselves. Consideration should be made for a careful search of the home and outbuildings. This course of action is most important with the full co-operation of the parents, as it is unwise to carry out extended searches outside the locus with a vastly increased police presence if the answer is at home. The age of the missing child is very important, especially if the child is of an immature age or, if older, has there been any evidence of boy-girl romance? Are there further children of the family? What is their demeanour, appearance or general well-being? It is not suggested for one moment that the family may not appear affluent and that the children have been badly treated. Once the first visiting officer has made all the initial enquiries he will immediately pass his observations to his supervisors so that higher authority will take further action, especially if the first officer has registered his views that all is not well. If the missing child has not been found within a responsible period of time the senior ranks will decide an appropriate course of action. More personnel will be drafted into the area and every officer must be informed of the circumstances and provided with a full description of the missing child.

## Murder of Julie Mary Bradshaw, 10 years old, Skelmersdale, 1970

The necessity for the aforementioned course of action was highlighted by the murder of a ten-year-old girl, Julie Mary Bradshaw, at Skelmersdale in Lancashire, in February 1970. At 7:30 p.m. on 4 February a telephone call was received at the police station from a father worried that his 10-year-old daughter was missing from home, and that she had a mental age of five years. A local police constable visited the house and his immediate assessment was that all was not well and he registered concern for the missing girl. He obtained the necessary details to pass to his supervisors and circulated the information. A full scale search for the missing girl was commenced and the house and surrounding area searched with the assistance of members of the neighbourhood. In view of the child's mental age, great concern was expressed for her welfare and the area was surrounded by a considerable number of police officers for the rest of the day and night.

The circumstances were that the missing girl left home at 4:30 p.m. to go to a nearby shop for groceries for her mother. The shop was on the same street as her home. She was known to have left the shop at about 4:50 p.m. and was seen in the road by a ten-year-old boy shortly afterwards. All weekend there was intense police activity in the area with a negative result. On Monday 9 February, I, and a district task force, were deployed to Skelmesdale and the search area extended. An incident control was set up in a local mission hall, and it was now believed that the missing girl was the subject of a serious crime. As enquiries continued, a lorry driver found part of the missing girl's clothing. He stated that the clothing was not where he had found it a short while before, indicating a local connection.

About 3:00 p.m. the same afternoon the police officer who first visited the home of the missing girl, visited the locality where the clothing had been found and nearby he saw a 14-year-old boy. The constable questioned him and was not satisfied with his explanation that he was curious about the found clothing and that he was only watching the police activity. The constable took the boy to the police control room and I allocated a detective sergeant to interview him. The youth was evasive and told lies about his activities. At that stage there was no direct information that he was a suspect concerning the missing girl. As a final process of elimination it was decided to search his home. At the conclusion of the search it was decided to examine the loft of the premises. The partly clothed body of the missing girl was found. A post mortem examination established that she had been strangled and also asphyxiated by drowning in a bucket of water. How he managed to carry out this terrible crime in his house which was on the same street walked by the missing girl and where his parents lived, will never be known. The important points regarding the murder of this girl are that the initial police officers who recorded the event did a first class job plus the fact that the area being the subject of intense police activity, prevented the body being removed and later discharged, possibly in circumstances that it would never be found.

A very similar case occurred in Flixton, Manchester, when a report was received that a young school girl had failed to return home from school. As in Skelmersdale the missing from home report was properly handled. The route that the missing girl would take home was examined and it was found that a garage proprietor had premises there. The owner was questioned by two detectives who did not like his demeanour. They informed their supervisors who gave instructions that he should be re-interviewed and his garage and home searched. During the course of the search at his home, one of the detectives saw what appeared to be a large bedding box. The owner was asked what it contained and he said bedding. The detective raised the lid, moved some of the contents and there found the body of the missing child in a large luggage carrier bag. Again, because the missing from home information was properly assessed along with the considerable police activity, the assailant was prevented from disposing of the body. He had arranged to do that at a suitable time and again, probably in circumstances which would mean that it would never be found. Both cases had sexual connections.

These two cases highlight what can be very difficult inquiries, but one of the most alarming factors to be observed is the different age groups of the assailants, from a young boy to a mature man – alarming to say the least. Even as I write this a case appeared in the local newspaper of a motorist trying to entice a young schoolgirl into his car. She refused but he persisted, got out of his car and caught hold of her. Fortunately she escaped. It is down to the general public to be aware of these activities and if suspicious circumstances are seen, to do something about it and inform the police. How things have changed over the years.

## Ill-treatment and death of children in domestic circumstances

The ill-treatment and death of children do not always occur as in the aforementioned circumstances. The police receive many reports of children being found dead in domestic circumstances, from doctors, visiting nurses, care workers, social workers and even from a member of the family.

I do not refer to the cot death syndrome but to cases, of which there are many, of apparent ill-treatment leading to the death of children and resulting in much distress to family and friends. Evidence is always apparent at post mortems when injuries consist of cuts, bruises, broken bones (new or old), and internal injuries leading to death. On reports being received, police visits to homes sometimes reveal that all is not well when observing other members of the family or the domestic circumstances in general. It is only in sometimes exceptional circumstances that the comment, 'how can people live like that?' is appropriate. Men and women are sometimes not fit to have children.

On 2 October 1973 I was informed of the death of a young female child at Burnley under suspicious circumstances. At the post mortem it was established that the child had died through a multitude of injuries inflicted with force to various parts of the body including head, chest and arms, not all of recent origin. It transpired that the mother of the deceased had three other children whose ages ranged from three to seven, and she lived with her boyfriend at her home. I interviewed the mother at Burnley Police Station and questioned her regarding her child's death. She admitted that she had chastised her children by smacking their bottoms when the need arose, but no more than that. She mentioned that her children were always fighting one another and that on a previous occasion the deceased had a broken arm, which received medical attention. She denied that she had hit her children with such force as to cause bruising. She admitted that her deceased daughter had an injury to the forehead which the other children said was caused by falling out of bed. I queried the relationship with her boyfriend and the children. She said that he was strict with them and punished them by putting them to bed early. I explained that some of the injuries which had killed her daughter were violent blows to the stomach. She denied having inflicted them.

I interviewed the boyfriend on two occasions. During the first interview he denied all knowledge of how the child had died by insisting that the children were always fighting and had jumped on the deceased's stomach. Having made further enquiries I interviewed him again and informed him that I knew that he was alone with the children on the Saturday night before the child's death. He admitted that he had heard the deceased child crying so he went to her bedroom and bedded her down. I challenged him that when he went upstairs the other children heard him slap her and beat her. The questioning continued and it became obvious that he was becoming agitated and clenched his fists and began to shake. He then admitted that he had inflicted the blows that killed the child. He explained that she had messed the bed and, as he could not stand dirt, he lost control and lashed out at her, causing her death. I examined the deceased child's bed and found that the centre of her mattress had rotted away. When the accused appeared at Lancaster Assize Court I took the mattress as an exhibit. The judge was not very happy with the unsightly piece of bedding but it told its own story. The boyfriend was sentenced to ten years in prison for manslaughter.

There are many other examples of ill-treatment and causing the death of children. In 1969 I was a detective inspector at Accrington when I received a report of the sudden death of a newly born male child. There seemed to be no apparent reason for the death so a post mortem was carried out. The cause of death was established, suffocation caused by pieces of paper being stuffed down the baby's throat. There had also been a plastic bag placed over the baby's head. The young mother was in hospital and I interviewed her there. She explained that she had been alone when she gave birth in her bathroom and she placed the plastic bag over its head to prevent blood staining. She also admitted that she wiped the baby with toilet roll and must have pushed some down its throat. A tragic case of a girl trying to conceal that she had been pregnant from her parents. Her sentence was probation for the offence of concealing a birth.

There are many strange cases regarding children. In 1967 at Morecambe, a couple who longed for children but were unsuccessful were at the stage of considering adoption. One night, on securing the front door of their home for the evening, they heard a noise outside. On investigating they found what appeared to be a newly born baby under a bush, wrapped in a shawl, with a note to the effect that your wish is granted. I went to the scene and found that the baby was wearing clothing with a name printed thereon. The name was quickly traced and it was found that the clothing had been owned by more than one mother and passed on through sales. The mother was quickly traced and at first stated that she had given her baby for adoption to a couple who took it away by car. She then admitted that she did not want the child but knew of a couple who wanted a family, so she left it outside their house. These cases are usually dealt with by a court with a sympathetic sentence.

In 1972 I dealt with a similar type of case in Darwen. A dog walker exercising his dog on some spare land found the body of what appeared to be a newly born baby. It had been there for some time in hot weather. A ligature was wound around its throat. Some two weeks after the body was found, and after considerable enquiries, I saw a young girl at her home. It was suspected that some time recently she had been pregnant. She denied having abandoned the child but admitted that she had recently had an abortion in the toilet at her home. She agreed to be medically examined, after which her father informed me that she had a child in the bathroom of their home and had afterwards abandoned the body. She admitted being responsible but, because of her age, she did not realise she was pregnant until the baby was born. She stated that she was frightened and did not know what to do. She also admitted that she had wrapped a sanitary towel around its neck. She finally confirmed the case by declaring the true sex of the baby. This was another distressing case for the family which was dealt with in the usual manner at court.

# SEVEN

# Murder of Alan Kenyon
## Bolton, 13 December 1970

ON SUNDAY 13 DECEMBER 1970, a bachelor, 37-year-old Alan Kenyon, was murdered at his cottage in Harwood, Bolton. It was quite obvious that he was financially sound from the quality of the furniture and fittings. There was no forced entry into the premises, indicating that the assailant was either a friend or had been invited inside. Early on 14 December I and many other detectives were summoned by the deputy head of CID, Superintendent Alf Collins, to attend a murder control near to the scene to commence enquiries. Superintendent Collins surveyed the house and after the body had been removed I, along with the various specialists following the normal procedure, visited the house to get a proper feel for the incident. We were aware that the deceased had been found naked, lying face down on a bed. There was very little disturbance or blood staining to say the deceased had been struck several heavy blows to the back of the head and neck. He also had defence wounds to his hands. The weapon used was a heavy poker, which had been left at the scene.

Set in a good area of Bolton, Kenyon's home was a well-established bachelor's accommodation. He was well known in the area as a party lover who frequently invited men of a similar mode in life as himself back to his home for drinks and sexual adventures. He worked locally in his family business as a confectioner. It may have appeared that his life style would not have attracted violence, but experience has shown that homosexuals can be exploited, or even attacked and robbed by violent criminals who consider them easy victims. It was, therefore, one line of enquiry to be followed. I had in the past been involved with the murder of a homosexual in Blackburn. When the body was examined it was found that he concealed his currency notes inside his shoes, indicating and later confirming that people of that way of life were being exploited, robbed and threatened that if they informed the police they would be subject to further violence.

As forensic scientists examined the lounge of Kenyon's home they found two sets of underpants – one of a floral pattern of quality material and the other pair of a string-vest type of material. Three drinking glasses were found on a table, suggesting that three persons were present at the same time. Also found in the room was a pistol-shaped cigarette lighter. A left-hand glove was found to have held the poker but it was doubtful that it had been worn. The other glove was found in a drawer, raising the possibility that a search had been made. An assumption could be made that the assailant was not a homosexual but had agreed to partake up to a certain stage in order to commit theft or take some other advantage.

Detective Superintendent Collins briefed the assembled detectives regarding the circumstances of Kenyon's death and investigating teams were set up, including house-to-house, background and *modus operandi*. I took charge of the follow-up enquiries squad. It was quickly established that the deceased had picked up at least two youths that night and had taken them to his home. They stated that they left about 9:00 p.m. and at that time Kenyon was still alive. Kenyon had left his home again seeking further male company, which may have transpired to be his killer.

I remained at the murder control until 17 December, when a forensic science report was received indicating that the string-vest type underpants found at the murder scene had not been worn by the deceased and that there was a printed name tab sown onto the garment. Simple enquiries at the appropriate department revealed that a doctor of that name was employed at the Royal Preston Hospital. I was dispatched there with a team of detectives to follow the valuable evidence. The doctor at Preston was interviewed and shown the relevant pair of underpants. He immediately identified them as his property and explained that whilst at university his mother had sewn a name tab on all his clothing. This left him in an extremely precarious position until he explained that someone had broken into the laundry at the infirmary and had stolen his and other people's clothing. Crime records at Preston confirmed that between 7 and 9 March the laundry had been forcibly entered and clothing stolen.

*Picture from one of the local papers covering the story*

● Det Chief Insp. Hunter with some of his team of 12 picked men examines the side window of the laundry at Preston Royal Infirmary through which the thief is believed to have entered.

The connection between Bolton and Preston raised considerable press interest. In order to trace witnesses or receive information regarding the burglary at the laundry, a front page article was published by the Lancashire Evening Post highlighting the point of entry. The circumstances were peculiar. What type of individual would break in to a laundry and steal someone else's clothes? And, still be wearing the garments in December, nine months after the burglary?

Whilst examining crime records and having consultations with local detectives at Preston a local who had been a prolific burglar came to my notice. He was currently in custody in Walton prison, Liverpool. He could not have been involved with the murder in Bolton because he was in custody at the time. Nevertheless, with Detective Sergeant Cyril Johnstone who had dealt with this individual before, we went to Walton prison and interviewed him. We were able to examine the clothing he was wearing and other articles kept in storage for him, with a negative result. It was obvious to me that the detective sergeant and the criminal were on talkative terms. He admitted that he had been extremely active committing crime and had been sentenced appropriately. From that interview the detective sergeant formed a conclusion as to who his criminal associates might be, even though he never admitted any.

A further records search was carried out at Preston which revealed further suspects, and a local criminal, Gordon Leonard Lee became apparent. A further search revealed that he had appeared at court and was in prison at the time of the murder. One aspect of murder investigation is to be a non-believer until the facts have been proved. A check at the prison he was being held in indicated that at the approximate time of the murder he was regarded as an escapee, having failed to return to jail from home leave. Lee had many previous convictions for a variety of offences. In 1964 whilst an absconder from an approved school, he and his brother became involved in a

*Alan Kenyon wearing a toupée. Murdered December 1970*

serious fight with four Pakistanis. In the course of the fight his brother was killed. He had convictions for robbery with violence, attacking a 37-year-old woman with a knife and snatching her handbag. He was a man of violence.

Considering his past history and the violence used to kill Kenyon Lee, he became number one candidate for examination or arrest. I obtained a search warrant and along with colleagues visited his home in Preston. Our introduction to the entry of the premises was given by two vicious Alsatian dogs. We were not deterred and gained entry. Several members of the family were present but appeared subdued. We informed Lee's parents why we were there and then searched the premises. Several locations met with a negative result. The family was

seated in the kitchen. A further search was conducted –
in that room there was a pottery sink which was mounted
on a small two-door cupboard. A detective opened the
door whereupon a voice called out, 'you have got to try
haven't you?' Lee was wrapped around the waste pipe
under the sink. He was arrested and taken to Preston
Police Station. I telephoned the murder control at Bolton
and informed them of the details of the arrest along with
details of the offender.

Shortly afterwards I received a call that Lee's
fingerprints had been found inside Kenyon's home. He
was taken to the murder control in Bolton where, on
being interviewed, he admitted the murder and made a
confession statement. He also admitted that he had stolen
two coats from Kenyon's home. Lee stated that on leaving
the premises he realised he had left behind his underwear
and his gun-shaped cigarette lighter.

He admitted that he had been picked up by Kenyon on
the 13 December and taken to his home, two other youths
left the premises. He admitted that Kenyon had made
sexual advances towards him and asked him to stay the
night. He agreed, as he was on the run and had nowhere
else to go. Kenyon gave him a drink and, as he took his
shirt off, made a grab for him. Lee pushed him away but
Kenyon would not stop so he hit him with a poker. There
was no mention of where the murder took place, but the
murder scene indicated that Kenyon was naked, face
down on the bed, in a passive homosexual mode.

There was no suggestion that Lee had homosexual
tendencies, but being on the run from prison he took
advantage of accommodation and provisions. His
background certainly indicated he was a man of violence,
quite capable of committing murder.

At Manchester Crown Court after a three-day trial for
murder to which he pleaded not guilty, he was sentenced
to life imprisonment plus two years for stealing the two
coats. Mr Justice Cusack on sentencing Lee said: 'it is
plain that you are a violent and dangerous man, this

crime in which you battered an unfortunate victim is unhappily in keeping with your character and is totally inexcusable.'

The case of Alan Kenyon illustrated how vulnerable certain members of the community can be. He seemed to be oblivious to the danger he was placing himself in. He was not a youngster but a mature 37-year-old, an apparently extremely active homosexual, who was prepared to walk the streets and pick up a complete stranger for sexual exploits. There are always criminals who will exploit any situation for financial gain.

# EIGHT

# Murder of Elizabeth Margaret Foster

## Kirkham, 4 January 1972

ON 4 JANUARY 1972, A telephone call was received at Kirkham Police Station, Lancashire, from a distressed parent saying that his daughter, Elizabeth Foster, was missing from home. About three hours later another telephone call was received from a land owner, to the effect that the body of a young girl had been found on his land. It was Elizabeth and she had been brutally strangled.

This was the murder of a seventeen-year-old Sunday school teacher, which transpired to be a forensic science classic committed by a sexual predator.

Elizabeth Foster was the only child of a deeply religious family who lived in Kirkham. She had recently returned home from a five day holiday at a Christian study centre in Carnforth, Lancashire. Her usual practice was to travel to Preston on Sunday nights to attend the Pentecostal church on North Road. She usually caught a bus from Kirkham around 5:30 p.m., arriving at Preston at about 6:30 p.m. where she met her friends. There was a suggestion that she sometimes accepted a car lift provided she knew the driver. She was known to have attended Kirkham Methodist Church Sunday school on the morning of 2 January 1972. Later the same day she left home about 5:33 p.m. to catch the bus at Millbanke bus stop, Kirkham, for Preston. En route she was accompanied by a female friend, but they parted company before the bus stop. Another male witness who knew Elizabeth slightly said that he saw her walking along the road and stop at the bus stop.

The bus which Elizabeth should have caught left Blackpool approximately ten minutes late and did not arrive at Kirkham until about 5:50 p.m. Three people who knew Elizabeth, one of whom was on the bus from Blackpool and the other two were waiting for the same bus at Kirkham, said that Elizabeth did not get on the bus to Preston. The conclusions were that someone must have picked her up at the bus stop at about 5:40–5:45 p.m. A female friend, who had been with Elizabeth at the study centre in Carnforth, waited for her in Preston on the Sunday night but she did not arrive. Elizabeth did not return home that night, but her parents were not particularly worried because she sometimes stayed with relatives in Preston. However, when she had not returned home by lunchtime the following day they reported that she was missing from home to the police.

Elizabeth was known as a quiet shy girl. She loved animals and a neighbour mentioned that she used to go

*Elizabeth Margaret Foster Murdered Kirkham, 1972*

to their house and play with puppies which they used to breed. They knew her well and although she was very attractive they did not believe that she ever had a serious boyfriend. She was devoted to her parents and the church. The minister at Kirkham Methodist Church had known her for two and a half years, and indicated that she held offices as a Sunday school teacher and secretary of the juvenile mission association. She played the piano for Sunday school and the youth fellowship, and the church organ on occasions. She was bright at school, gaining several 'O' levels and studying for three 'A' level certificates. She was hoping to study for a degree course in Social Sciences.

Elizabeth's body was found on a dirt track off Bryning Avenue, Wrea Green near Kirkham. The head of Lancashire CID, Detective Chief Superintendent Joe Mounsey, took charge of the investigation and held police and press conferences on 4 January 1972. He set up a murder control in Kirkham and summoned a team of some one hundred detectives to carry out enquiries.

A post mortem confirmed that she had been strangled and sexually assaulted. A forensic analysis of samples removed from the body concluded that the assailant was of blood group 'B' secretor. In those days we relied on blood groups as we did not have the developed benefit of DNA. The establishment of the assailant's blood was most important as it is a fairly uncommon group, relating to a minority of the population. Other forensic science examinations of Elizabeth's clothing revealed flecks of pillar box red paint, red car carpet fibres and minute samples of vehicle upholstery. Because we had been able to establish the assailant's blood group, as the inquiry progressed it was decided to endeavour to obtain saliva samples from every male person of mature age in the Kirkham area, under fifty years being the norm. The technique used was the provision of large quantities of small glass bottles into which the males were asked to spit. The contents would then be forensically analysed; a massive task. The only similar task undertaken was in 1948 when a murder was committed in Blackburn and the mammoth task of fingerprinting the male population of the town was undertaken, ultimately with a positive result.

As enquiries continued into the murder, the immediate area of intense activity was where the body had been found and on the road where she would normally have caught the bus to Preston. House-to-house enquiries began and people who had been on the road at the material time were interviewed in depth. Information came to light regarding vehicles seen, and it became necessary to establish a vehicle squad for the reason that she must have been picked up and offered a lift to Preston. In particular, witnesses referred to a Mini motor car, the colour of which was stated as being bronze, yellow or mustard, but later described as a 'Mini GT saffron coloured'. This car was thought to have stopped near the bus stop with two men on board. The vehicle was heard to be revved up and drove away at speed. One witness who saw the vehicle also saw a young girl, whom she did not know, standing at the bus stop, but she did not see her getting into the vehicle.

The main areas of enquiry were

- The tracing of vehicles with the assistance of the D.V.L.C. (Driver and Vehicle Licencing Centre)

- The tracing of males who had the 'B' blood group

- The examination of the scene where the body was found

The area was well known in the village of Wrea Green as a 'courting couples' place of resort', and was used by people of that type regularly. The rough lane was immediately secured and the track itself was covered by plastic sheets so that a thorough examination could be made. Extensive enquiries were made to trace people who frequented the location. This included local people who exercised their dogs, in fact two people following their daily routine actually found the body of Elizabeth Foster. The time would be approximately two hours after lunch time on Monday 3 January. Thorough examinations were carried out before the body was moved. Part of her clothing was missing including underwear, a shoe and a purse. Searches were carried out by foot patrols and by army personnel from a nearby military camp using metal detectors in the surrounding fields.

*Map of Kirkham and the surrounding area*

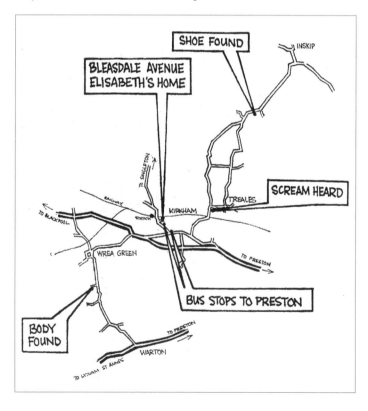

On Monday 3 January 1972 a retired driver living in Inskip, some distance from Kirkham, was walking in the area when he found a black patent leather shoe lying in a ditch. In a field close to the one where he found the shoe, he found a pair of ladies' briefs. A witness reported hearing a female scream near to where the items were found. He took both items home, showed them to his wife and burnt them. He was later shown the shoe found near Elizabeth Foster's body and stated that they were similar. He removed the ashes from his fire and handed them to a detective – the buckles from the ashes were proved to be similar to the other shoe recovered.

Information was received that on two previous occasions Elizabeth was observed at her usual bus stop in Kirkham at approximately 5:30 p.m. when an ordinary saloon car, driven by a mature man, flashed his headlights and then stopped. The driver opened the door; Elizabeth got in and was driven away towards Kirkham town centre. An appeal was made for this person to come forward but there was a negative result.

On 30 January 1972 a Blackpool tram driver was walking with his family on Lee Road, Marton, some considerable distance from Kirkham, when he found a purse submerged in water. He recovered it and handed it over to the police. It was duly identified as Elizabeth's property. The findings of the shoe, briefs and now the purse confirmed that the assailant had been travelling different routes discarding the items found in his vehicle after disposing of Elizabeth's body.

On 10 January 1972 an inquest was opened into the death of Elizabeth Foster. The cause of death was given as asphyxia. On 13 January her funeral was held. The cortège left her home in Bleasdale Avenue, Kirkham, and the service was conducted at the Methodist church, Elizabeth's usual place of worship. Both the church and the nearby church hall were full to capacity. Loudspeakers were installed in the church hall so that the service could be relayed. More than fifty wreaths and floral tributes garlanded the coffin. Crowds gathered outside the church and along the route taken by the funeral cortège. It was a massive event with the whole of Kirkham in mourning.

Massive police enquiries continued with teams of detectives assigned to trace *modus operandi* suspects (similar offenders) for elimination. Vehicle owners known to be in the area were asked to account for their movements or to provide any information they may have.

Some eleven weeks into the inquiry I was instructed by Detective Chief Superintendent Mounsey to visit the murder control and review the mountain of paperwork accumulated by over a hundred detectives. Thirty-five thousand people had been seen, over 10,250 male saliva samples had been analysed, 626 soldiers had been interviewed, 5,160 statements had been taken, 3,588 telephone messages had been received, 6 anonymous letters and phone calls had been received and there was an index of 500,000 vehicles in the system. I very quickly found that the main suspect vehicle, a saffron-coloured Mini GT, had been traced and the occupants eliminated. The next most important matter to be examined was to find the vehicle which had been used by the assailant. I examined the outstanding list of males who had not yet provided a saliva sample. I found that a nearby farmer had so far, after several attempts, failed to provide a sample. My instructions to the two detectives were quite simple – go and get it and don't come back without it. The two detectives returned waving the required sample, but it was observed that their pin striped suits were splattered with mud. They explained that on speaking to the farmer's wife she pointed out a nearby field, telling them that's where they would find him. The farmer was ploughing and refused to stop on being requested. The detectives had no option but to run over the ploughed field and jump up onto the tractor. One held the steering wheel whilst the other held the glass bottle to the farmer's mouth with gave the instruction to spit. Mission accomplished without the tractor stopping – dedication to duty. The sample was negative.

I found that the forensic scientists had done a very thorough examination of the scene where the body had been found, to the extent that plaster casts had been made of the tyre impressions. Two of the tyres' treads were of Fisk manufacture whilst the other two were Dunlop. They also deduced that the dimensions of the car corresponded to a Morris Oxford type of car, this valuable information, coupled with the samples of pillar box red paint and the red fibres recovered from the victim's clothing, meant only one thing: the suspect vehicle was a red coloured Morris Oxford type of vehicle. With renewed vigour I briefed a team of detectives to go and find the vehicle. I highlighted the possibility that because of the length of the investigation, the killer may have scrapped or otherwise disposed of the vehicle. They were instructed to visit every scrap yard on the Fylde coast.

Within a short time Detective Sergeant Ray Hodges and Detective Constable Don Cooper informed me that they had found a suspect vehicle in a scrap yard in Poulton-Le-Fylde, a short distance from Kirkham. The yard had many scrap vehicles piled on top of one another, including many Morris Oxford types. The one of interest was a red MG saloon car, registration PCK 53, with a similar dimension to a Morris Oxford type. It was pillar box red in colour although a crude attempt had been made to cover part of the body work with black paint. The vehicle carpets were red with decaying upholstery. The complete set of tyres and wheels were missing. The two detectives made enquiries and recovered three of the missing wheels and tyres. Two of them were of Dunlop manufacture and the other was a Fisk. A plaster cast had been made from the track used to dispose of Elizabeth's body and I compared the cast alongside the Fisk tyre. I found that at some time the tyre had been punctured and a rubber plug had been inserted. That plug was also apparent in the plaster cast, conclusive proof that this recovered car was the one used to deposit Elizabeth Foster's body.

The car had been more or less reduced to a shell. In addition to the missing wheels, many other fittings were absent. The vehicle was transported to the North West Forensic Science Laboratory where its complete history was established, including previous ownership.

The owner of the vehicle during the time when Elizabeth Foster was murdered was quickly traced and a sample of his saliva analysed as a 'B' secretor. He was arrested on 28 April and made two admission statements. He had been employed as a bus conductor by a Blackpool company which used the route normally taken by Elizabeth Foster from Kirkham to Preston. Initial enquiries revealed that on the night of 2 January 1972 he should have been employed on that bus route according to his work records, but it was revealed that he was given four hours off. Many times in the past he must have been on duty on the Kirkham–Preston route during a Sunday night and befriended Elizabeth. On the fatal night, his last minute request for time off combined with having to find a replacement may have caused the bus to be late to

*Below and right: Recovery of the vehicle used to transport Elizabeth to her death*

Kirkham. He had obviously planned to pick her up in his car as he knew her usual movements, and she may have considered him as a friend.

Brian Herbert Ball duly appeared at Lancaster Castle Crown Court in October 1972, when he pleaded not guilty to the murder of Elizabeth Foster. In his admission statement he indicated that he knew Elizabeth through his employment as a bus conductor and that he had mentioned to her that he would pick her up by car and take her to Preston. However he deviated from his route and on stopping his vehicle they started 'necking'. It was only when he attempted to go further that she started screaming and kicking. He admitted that he put his hand on her neck to prevent her screaming. Forensic science proved that sexual intercourse took place either before or after she died. At the beginning of the trial at Lancaster he attempted to change his plea of not guilty to murder to guilty to manslaughter. This was not accepted by the prosecution and a trial proceeded. He was found not guilty of murder but guilty of manslaughter. The judge sentenced him to ten years in prison; a similar sentence to a murder verdict.

Brian Herbert Ball was undoubtedly a sexual predator with designs on an innocent and respectable member of the community in Kirkham. His sentence should have been life imprisonment.

Detective Sergeant Ray Hodges and Detective Constable Don Cooper were highly commended by the judge for excellent detective work.

# NINE

# Blackpool Victoria Hospital:
## the murder of three children and attempted murder of two nurses
## 17 February 1972

THIS WAS A MOST HORRIFIC murder when three children were stabbed to death on a children's ward of a hospital. They had been sent for medical treatment by an ophthalmic surgeon actually employed at the hospital. The initial investigation only lasted one day, resulting in very little press or media attention. The assailant duly appeared at a Crown Court where he was adjudged to be in such a mental state that he was unfit to plead to any of the preferred charges.

Four children were detained on a ward at Blackpool Victoria Hospital on the night of 17 February 1972. The ward was being supervised by two nurses. One of the children had been a little unruly and had a wide mesh net placed over its cot to prevent the child climbing out and injuring himself. Everything appeared normal during the evening until just after midnight when the nurses became aware of a disturbance on the ward. They found a male person attacking the children. He had not been seen entering the premises and the attack was frenzied, with repeated blows being rained on the children. The two nurses immediately tried to intervene only to be subjected to several blows themselves. It was then that the nurses realised the assailant was in possession of a knife. Both nurses received life threatening injuries and it was fortunate that they were in hospital and received immediate medical attention. Had this not been the case, the end result would have been very different. In the meanwhile the assailant made good his escape and was only seen briefly by another member of staff. That night Sergeant Bob Dobson and another constable were already at the hospital casualty department as they called in on a routine nightly basis. They were speaking to staff when information of the incident was received. Sergeant Dobson was first at the horrific scene and sought immediate help to search the area. He alerted Detective Superintendent Saunders and reinforcements were immediately drafted in.

One of the first police officers to arrive at the hospital was a member of the police's alien department. On hearing of the brief description of the assailant he arrived at hospital with a quantity of photographs. One of the badly injured nurses was being prepared for an operation. Although unable to speak, on being shown a photograph she indicated a part identification of the individual who had been her attacker. That photograph was of Dr Ahamad Alami, an ophthalmic surgeon employed at Blackpool Victoria Hospital.

A large contingency of police officers was dispatched to the scene and sealed the whole area, led by Chief Constable Bill Palfray, who did not do things by half measures.

An examination of the children's ward revealed an horrific scene, three children stabbed to death and a fourth badly injured with his life in danger. On examination of the cot with the wide mesh net attached an important piece of evidence came to light in the form of a cuff link with a Middle-Eastern design, found in the cot bed covers. It had apparently been dislodged in the course of a stabbing motion through the net.

Dr Alami, who lived in accommodation across the road from the hospital, was heard by neighbours returning to his room late on the night of 17 February and was heard to spend a lot of time running water, obviously washing blood from his hands and clothing. He was duly arrested and his room searched, where a cuff link identical to the one recovered from the net covered cot was found. A knife of similar dimensions to that used in the attacks was also found.

When arrested it became obvious that all was not well with his mental state, but he had had the presence of mind after the murders to attempt to cover his tracks by washing away the blood staining. How could a doctor of his stature be responsible for such brutal conduct in committing one of the most horrible crimes ever perpetrated in Lancashire?

On examination of hospital records, it was revealed that Dr Alami had already been examined by a Blackpool Victoria psychiatrist, and had been assessed as being a paranoid schizophrenic in a precarious condition. This diagnosis was apparently considered unethical and it was recommended that Alami should be reassessed by an independent psychiatrist. At the time of the murders this had not been done.

Dr Alami had legitimate access to Blackpool Victoria Hospital but his work did not extend to visits to the children's ward. His responsibilities were confined to mainly eye surgery in a different part of the hospital. Extensive work was required to prove that Dr Alami was responsible for the attacks in the children's ward. Invaluable work was done by forensic science, leading to positive conclusions. A shoe impression which matched the doctor's was found alongside one of the cots.

Both nurses recovered fully from their injuries, and I have no doubt that in the course of time would have identified their assailant. Fortunately sufficient evidence was immediately available to arrest him and possibly prevent further atrocious acts being committed.

Dr Alami duly appeared at Crown Court where it was determined that, because of his mental state, he was unfit to plead to the various charges against him. His background was carefully researched and it was confirmed that he was a Jordanian with a degree from a university in Egypt. His father was a high ranking 'Mufti' (religious leader) in Jerusalem. It was also established that he had been discharged from the Jordanian Army medical corps in 1970, as a paranoid schizophrenic. He came to England soon afterwards and obtained a medical position at a London hospital before making his move to Blackpool. It seems to indicate that few checks had been made into his background when he arrived in the UK. After his court appearance he spent several years in Broadmoor high security hospital before being deported to the Middle East.

In the year 2000 Dr Alami applied for a visa to return to the UK to study for a Ph.D. in political science in London. He stated that he was now cured of his mental illness and wanted to apologise to the families of his victims. An initial application was rejected, but in a move likely to bring furious criticism of British immigration laws, a second visa request was considered by a Home Office review tribunal, before being rejected.

The reasons for Dr Alami's behaviour were never explained. It is a tragic fact that both diagnoses of paranoid schizophrenia, in Jordan and in Blackpool, were not acted upon. Had they been, the horrific murder of three children would have been avoided.

# TEN

# The 'Black Panther' murder cases

THIS BECAME ONE OF THE most enormous murder inquiries ever conducted by Lancashire Constabulary in its history. I was staff officer to Detective Chief Superintendent Joe Mounsey from 6 September 1974 until 18 February 1975.

In addition to Derek Astin, Donald Neilson, the Black Panther (so named by pressmen because of his attire) murdered Donald Skepper, a sub-postmaster, at Harrogate, Yorkshire, on Friday 15 February 1974, and Sidney Grayland on 11 November 1974 at Langley sub-Post Office, Oldbury, Birmingham. The panther then went on to kidnap and murder Lesley Whittle, an heiress at Beech Croft, Highley, Shropshire, on Tuesday 14 January 1975.

## The Murders of Derek Astin and Donald Skepper, Baxenden and Harrogate, 1974

The Baxenden sub-Post Office, a combined mixed grocery business of a dormer bungalow construction, was occupied by Derek Astin, his wife and two children. About 4:00 a.m. on 6 September 1974, Mrs Astin was awakened by her husband. On looking towards the bedroom door she saw a masked figure dressed in dark clothing. Mr Astin got out of bed and bundled the dark figure out of the room. The assailant retaliated and discharged a 12 bore shotgun causing a grievous wound to Mr Astin's left shoulder. The struggle continued on the staircase and Mr Astin was again shot with a .22 firearm. The assailant then made good his escape. Mr Astin's ability to defend himself was restricted because of a recent operation to an injured foot and legs. The emergency services were alerted and Mr Astin was taken to Accrington Victoria Hospital where he was found to be dead on arrival.

On arrival of the police and forensic science personnel it was found that entry had been gained to the premises through a rear living room window using a 'brace and bit' method to release the transom catch. The assailant had escaped back through the same window. An inquiry murder control post was set up at Accrington Police Station with over one hundred detectives, crime patrols, dog handlers and members of the regional crime squads. Initial information regarding the murder and the method of entry etc. were circulated to all neighbouring forces. We were immediately made aware of the murder of Donald Skepper, a sub-postmaster at Harrogate on 15 February 1974. A similar method of entry was gained

*Black Panther Murder Control, Accrington 1974*

to these premises; again the killer was dressed in black tight-fitting clothing and a mask. Liaison was established between the two police forces with an exchange of personnel. Similar to the Astins, Mr Skepper and his wife were in bed. They were awakened by their son who had earlier been bound and gagged, and sent into their bedroom for the post office safe keys. Mr Skepper made a move to get out of bed as if to rebel against the masked intruder and was immediately shot dead with a 12 bore shot gun. Both murders involved a ruthless killer who again made good his escape.

Extensive enquiries were made by both North Yorkshire and Lancashire Constabularies, and it became more and more apparent that both crimes were committed by the same individual. Indeed it transpired that break-ins to sub-post offices extended over a wide area:

> Sub-Post Office, Wentworth Road, Jump,
> Barnsley. 3:50 a.m., 6-1-1971

> Sub-Post Office, Kilnhurst Road, Rawmarsh,
> Rotherham. 4:30 a.m., 19-1-1971

> Sub-Post Office, Bury Hill Lane, Mansfield,
> Notts. 3:00 a.m., 31-3-1971

> Sub-Post Office, Rochdale Road East,
> Heywood. 4:00 a.m., 16-2-1972

> Sub-Post Office, Wortley Road, High Green,
> Sheffield. 3:55 a.m., 31-1-1973

In all these cases entry was gained by boring holes near catches then climbing through opened windows. In four cases the occupants were roused. They were tied up, the keys for the safe obtained and the contents removed. At the Heywood case the sub-postmaster got out of bed and struggled with the intruder in the course of which a 12 bore shotgun was discharged into the ceiling of the bedroom. The struggle continued down the staircase and the intruder escaped.

In addition to these five identical offences many more were committed in both Yorkshire and Lancashire. It became obvious that in addition to his method of entry, the intruder made his way into bedrooms and, if undisturbed, stole the post master's trousers in an effort to find the safe keys. On other occasions he displayed a certain amount of passion to the bound female members who suffered discomfort, but in the main it was apparent that he was an extremely fit, agile and ruthless individual. The majority of the sub-post office break-ins occurred on the Yorkshire side of the Pennines, indicating that the assailant came from there.

In view of the two weapons used in the Astin case, that is a 12 bore and a .22 calibre, it was assumed that the assailant had two different types of gun, but there was a possibility that he possessed a 'drilling' gun. This type of rifle has three barrels, twin 12 bore and a third barrel mounted under the 12 bore. The third barrel varies in calibre from .22 to .45 or even larger, referred to as an 'elephant' gun, used mainly by hunters when confronted by small or large animals. The use of such a weapon by the Black Panther was never confirmed; nevertheless enquiries into such a weapon were necessary.

In view of the type of premise being attacked the Royal Mail indicated that an award of £15,000 was available on an arrest. A top Royal Mail investigator was assigned to the murder control room at Accrington. Massive amounts of publicity pamphlets were delivered to the murder control in Accrington by the Royal Mail.

The difficulties of making the necessary enquiries throughout this large geographical area are obvious. Considering the likelihood that there is no local connection, there are definite complications in tracking down an offender responsible for a sequence of offences which have been committed in so many parts of the

North of England. All success in this type of inquiry must depend on communications, including the press, radio and television. Especially in view of this £15,000 reward. The inquiry so far is to be massively increased by further murders.

After twenty-four days Mr Mounsey released the following statement:

> The massive hunt continues for the killer of Derek Astin in Accrington. Twenty thousand people had been interviewed by a team of 130 detectives. It is possible that publicans, neighbours and possibly work mates could provide vital clues. The killer may have offered stamps or postal orders for sale cheaply, stolen from post office raids. He may be of smallish build, athletic, and buys that extra round of drinks and never explains why he is so flush with cash. Is he a neighbour with irregular habits, who often stays out all night without reason? Has he a wife or a girlfriend who must be suspicious of his activities? Is he an associate with an unusual interest in guns?
>
> Detectives have knocked on 9,000 doors. They have interviewed witnesses and taken 3,500 statements. The information obtained is being compared with 30,000 similar interviews carried out in Harrogate in relation to the similar murder of Donald Skepper. It is obvious that the same individual is responsible for both murders. Regional crime squad detectives are checking on raids on 120 sub-post offices in Lancashire and Yorkshire over the past four years. A considerable number of these premises have been attacked in a similar manner.
>
> The General Post Office and the National Federation of Sub-postmasters intend jointly to pay a reward of £15,000 for information which will lead to the arrest and conviction of the killer.

This special circulation failed to provide one snippet of information pointing in the Black Panther's direction, but it is suspected that the one person who knew of his activities was his wife. The Black Panther kept his own counsel and confided in no one.

## Murder of Sidney Grayland, November 1974

The Black Panther abandoned his attacks until 5:45 p.m. on 11 November 1974 at Oldbury, six miles from Birmingham. He attacked and shot dead Sidney Grayland, a sub-postmaster. Mr Grayland had closed his premises with his wife and was cashing up the day's takings when there was a knock at the door. On opening the door he was shot dead with a .22 weapon. His wife was also attacked and badly beaten with the same weapon, the butt of which splintered leaving a part at the scene. It was later identified as coming from a .22 revolver. Sidney Grayland's wife duly recovered and provided details of the attack. Again the assailant made good his escape.

Lancashire and Yorkshire Constabularies have no jurisdiction in the West Midlands, but it was decided that Det. Ch. Supt Mounsey and the head of CID in North Yorkshire, Det. Supt Dolby and myself should visit Oldbury on 14 January 1975 and liaise with the similar ranks there. The CID was made aware of attacks on sub-post offices in our area and we briefed them in the extent of our enquiries. No common factor came to light apart from sub-postmasters were being murdered. Reward money was now £25,000.

It was decided that all three police forces involved should hold a press conference in Dudley that day. This was arranged but we were amazed that very few press men arrived. We were told that another very serious incident had taken place in a nearby police area, just twelve miles away.

## Kidnapping and murder of Lesley Whittle, Tuesday 14 January 1975

Between 1:00 a.m. and 7:30 a.m. on Tuesday 14 January 1975, Lesley Whittle, an 18-year-old college student of Beech Croft, Highley, Shropshire, was kidnapped from her home. She was an heiress to a considerable amount of money held in trust until her 21st birthday, left by her deceased father who held considerable interests in a haulage and travel coach business. Lesley Whittle's parents parted in circumstances which aroused considerable press publicity. We were made aware of the kidnapping, but little did we believe that the circumstances would have any connection with the Black Panther. We did however attend the press conference regarding the kidnapping. On returning to Lancashire we maintained contact with the murder control room at Oldbury.

*Lesley Whittle's home from which she was kidnapped, 1975*

We were informed that at 10:30 p.m. on Wednesday 15 January 1975, a peculiar incident had taken place at the Freightliner depot in Dudley. A security guard had been shot seven times with a .22 gun by an assailant who had been acting suspiciously. An examination of the scene revealed that an attempt had been made to leave a message by securing pieces of Dymo tape (an adhesive tape) to a lamp standard.

An unbelievable turn of events now developed. Forensic scientists and ballistics experts shocked us all by announcing that the .22 bullet fired at Derek Astin, Sidney Grayland and the Freightliner guard had all come from the same gun. Even more important was that the securing of the Dymo tapes at the Freightliner depot was connected to the kidnapping of Lesley Whittle.

In all cases of kidnapping the most essential ingredient is complete co-operation between all the relevant authorities, including the press and media. A complete blackout of the circumstances is absolute. In the event of a leakage regarding the circumstances, the kidnapping can be exploited by criminals in a wide field and it becomes practically impossible to communicate with the perpetrator. The life of the victim is at stake, it is of such absolute importance.

A ransom note for £50,000 was left in the Whittle home. It included the words 'any tricks or police death'. The kidnapping case was led by Ch. Supt Bob Booth of West Mercia police. He held a press conference and highlighted the need for a complete blackout on information. However, a junior reporter leaked the details resulting in an explosion of press and media interest, and many false demands from would-be kidnappers. It also wasted a lot of valuable detective work.

The finding of the Dymo tape at Freightliners was the first attempt by the Panther to lay a trail of Dymo tapes in telephone kiosks, heading to an area to deposit the ransom money. More than one such trail was left for Lesley's brother, Ronald Whittle, to follow which entered into the

A Lancashire Constabulary artist's impression compiled from witnesses at Dudley who saw a man setting a Dymo trail, 1975.

realms of fantasy. Finally a trail was prepared which was to terminate in Bathpool Park at Kidsgrove, Staffordshire, 65 miles away from Highley in a telephone kiosk, again in Dymo tape. The time was in the early hours of the morning when the Panther assumed there would be no one there; a suitcase would be deposited near a flashing light. There was no co-operation between the West Mercia and the Staffordshire police. It became known that a car with a courting couple was in the park and a police vehicle also drove through the park. The deposit of the ransom money by Ronald Whittle was aborted. The Panther must have panicked and made good his escape.

Six days after the Kidsgrove incident a stolen car was found near the Freightliner depot. It was examined and found to contain a tape recorder with Lesley Whittle's voice thereon and many items of the Panther's tools of his criminal trade, including his dark-coloured hooded attire. It

*Ruthless killer Donald Neilson at the time of his arrest*

was suggested that the vehicle was parked in an exclusive heavy vehicle area and two lorry drivers parked on either side of the car so the doors could not be opened. The car was apparently parked as the Panther was laying his Dymo tape trail. He had no option but to abandon the vehicle.

The park at Kidsgrove was searched with a negative result, but because of tremendous media publication, members of the public began to surrender items they had found, including a torch, a tape recorder, a piece of Dymo tape discarded by the Panther, with the misspelled word 'suit care' instead of 'suit case'. Stafford police decided to carry out a thorough search of the park at Kidsgrove and found that the cover of an overspill drain was unbolted. On examining the drain the body of Lesley Whittle was found some 65 feet down. She was suspended by the neck by a multi-strand steel cable secured by U-bolts which could only to be released using a spanner.

On 11 December 1975 in Woodhouse, Nottinghamshire, two police officers were on duty in a police car when they saw a man acting suspiciously. They approached him, only to be confronted by the individual pointing a shot gun at them. He instructed them to get into the police car

and drive, with the words 'any tricks and you are dead'. As the police officer drove he was able to motion to his colleague that it was time for action. As he approached a fork in the road he jammed on the brakes and violently swung the vehicle. His colleague immediately grappled with the man and in the course of the struggle the shot gun was discharged inside the vehicle. All three of them stumbled onto the road. When a retired miner came to their assistance the assailant was arrested. Common, everyday police work achieved what thousands of hours of dedicated detective work could not. The Black Panther was caught in a similar manner to the Yorkshire Ripper – arrested by two police officers carrying out routine police work.

The Black Panther was in custody for two days before he would even disclose his name. It was however soon established that he was Donald Neilson, with an address in Bradford, West Yorkshire. After being interviewed by CID in Nottinghamshire he admitted the various murders he had committed. He made a long statement giving his version of the kidnapping and murder of Lesley Whittle. He stated that he first became interested in the Whittle family through the considerable press publicity regarding divorce proceedings between Lesley Whittle's parents. He decided that a considerable amount of money was available so he hatched the kidnapping plot. He must have spent a considerable amount of time in the area planning the event, which included visiting Bathpool Park, Kidsgrove, where he discovered the aforementioned rain drain. He fully admitted kidnapping Lesley Whittle whilst she was dressed only in night attire and slippers. He drove to Bathpool Park and took Lesley down into the rain drain. He had acquired a foam mattress and a sleeping bag which he arranged on a steel platform some distance below ground level. He then secured a steel cable around her neck and bolted the other end to the steel ladder. There was absolutely no way that she could escape without a spanner. He returned to the Highley area and made several attempts to lay trails using Dymo tape for the ransom money to be deposited. His final attempt to obtain the ransom money failed at Bathpool Park. He explained in his statement that he intended to release the girl even if the demand for money failed. He returned to the rain drain and descended the ladder. He saw that Lesley had her torch on and she moved slightly to allow him room to descend onto the platform, as she did so she fell off the platform suspended from the neck by the steel cable. He made no attempt to help her in anyway, clambered out of the drain and ran away.

Neilson's admission statement gave the impression that right from the start Lesley Whittle was in some way condoning his activities. How far from the truth can this be? An eighteen-year-old girl kidnapped from her own bed, dressed only in night clothes, taken down underground into a dark wet rain drain and tethered round her neck by a multi-strand steel rope secured by U-bolts using a spanner. Resting on a platform and a foam mattress and given the use of a sleeping bag. She was isolated there for days and it is impossible to assess the state of mind she must have been in. The cruelty of Neilson even exceeded his previous boundaries. There is little doubt that when his ransom demands failed he reverted to his previously displayed ruthless attitude and pushed Lesley Whittle off the platform to her death. If she had slipped off the platform as Neilson suggested, any normal human being would have immediately reacted and sprung to her assistance. He, of course, was not human. He was the Black Panther.

The arrest of Donald Neilson on 11 December 1975 created a considerable problem when a decision had to be made in relation to preparing court proceedings. The first murder was committed in February 1974, the second in September 1974, the third in November 1974, the attempted murder in January 1975 and the final murder of Lesley Whittle in January 1975. These murders were committed in four different police areas in England, all of which were prolonged, extensive investigations accumulating in many thousands of people being interviewed by each police force.

When arrested by the police he was again armed with a shot gun and there is little doubt that he had a further crime planned. If he had not contemplated further criminal activity he may never have been caught. Commander Morrison from New Scotland Yard, who had replaced Chief Superintendent Booth in the Lesley Whittle case, in his wisdom decided to deal with the various murders separately, and obtained an admission statement from Neilson regarding the kidnapping and murder of Lesley Whittle, obviously the most serious case involved. In actual fact the paperwork to support the various charges was limited in each case, compared with the number of statements taken during the various investigations. The essential task remained that each force would have to examine every statement taken to ensure that no evidence was apparent which could be used and would have to be passed on to Neilson's defence council as an entitlement.

On 21 July 1976 at Oxford Crown Court, Donald Neilson was given five life sentences. The judge, Mars-Jones, said: 'The enormity of your crimes puts you in a class apart from almost all convicted murderers. In your case life must mean life.' This brought an end to one of the most notorious killers in criminal history. Neilson was much influenced by his military training, displayed by the vast amount of terrorism material in his house. He displayed a complete disregard for the sanctity of human life.

The true extent of Donald Neilson's criminal activities will never be known. Many sub-postmasters may have been fortunate to have slept through their premises being broken into, only to later find that their safes had been emptied. The alternative does not bear thinking about.

The Black Panther, Donald Neilson, died in prison on 19 December 2011. I have no doubt that artefacts recovered after his arrest which were used in the course of his criminal career, will now be displayed in some police museums. However, only those who worked on the various cases can appreciate his extreme brutality and disregard for humanity.

# Murder of Janice McCallum
## Isle of Man, 31 May 1978

**THIS WAS THE MURDER OF a young girl on the Isle of Man by a sexual predator, a native of the island. She was on holiday with friends from Scotland. The incident occurred during the week of T.T. Races and the island's police resources were fully stretched, so the chief constable requested assistance from the Lancashire Constabulary.**

I prepared a team of detectives along with suitable equipment and on 2 June, accompanied by the head of CID, Detective Superintendent Brooks, travelled to Liverpool for a flight to the island. When we arrived at the airport we were informed that the flight was cancelled owing to the island being fog bound. The head of CID would not accept this and after considerable debate asked to see the pilot of the plane. The importance of our visit was spelt out. The pilot was amenable and he indicated that he also had passengers who wished to go to Belfast, so he agreed to make the journey at our own risk. The flight took off in complete silence. The pilot spoke on the intercom and explained to the other passengers that there were people on board who had to get to the Isle of Man, which was still fog bound, but he would attempt to land. He explained that if there was sudden violent acceleration, not to worry as this was normal if he had to abort the landing. As we approached the island all we could see was the top of Snaefell Mountain sticking out of the fog. The descent commenced through darkness, and then suddenly we had a clear view of the island accompanied by spontaneous applause. So much for health and safety. I would like to meet that pilot again and buy him a large glass of Scotland's famous brown liquid. An experienced detective sergeant getting off the plane exclaimed, 'I will never fly again'.

On arrival we were briefed by the chief constable regarding the circumstances of the murder and that it was extremely busy on the island owing to the T.T. races taking place at that time.

The murdered girl was Janice McCallum, a teenager on holiday from Scotland. On the evening of 31 May she, with friends, visited a hostelry frequented by young people in the capital, Douglas. A man assessed as maybe slightly older that herself showed interest in her and, according to friend, they seemed to be getting on well. They were thought to have left the premises together, but Janice did not arrive back at her accommodation that night. The following day, 1 June, her body was found in a garage, in a back street not far from the public house she had visited the night before. The local police visited the scene and it was obvious that she had been severely assaulted and that her clothing indicated a sexual attack. One of the first police officers on the scene, a local sergeant, found that in the course of the attack a quantity of cement powder had been spilled and there was a very distinct shoe pattern in it. The sergeant protected that impression for later forensic science examination. That impression was still there when I visited the scene and this transpired to become the most important exhibit leading to the detection of the murderer.

We introduced the Isle of Man CID to the Lancashire Constabulary system and arranged an intermixing of CID personnel. Very shortly the name of the man who had been seen in the company of the deceased on the night

*Murder of Janice McCallum, Isle of Man. Briefing of senior officers, 1978.*

of the 31st came to light, a further witness even saw the named man in the company of the deceased in the back lane near to where her body was found. Enquiries then revealed that the suspect, Michael Kelly aged twenty-two years, had committed suicide.

On 6 June, along with an Isle of Man detective chief inspector, I interviewed Kelly's wife and questioned her regarding her husband's movements on the night of 31 May. She had already made a statement to another detective and I queried the contents. In her statement she had said that her husband had arrived home when the ten o'clock news came on the TV. She admitted that she was reading a book and her concentration was on the book and not the TV. We informed her that her husband was seen in the back lane where the deceased had been found later than ten o'clock. Mrs Kelly, after a period of reflection, admitted that she could have been mistaken. We checked her bedroom and examined the clothing that she had referred to. She then made another statement recording her amended view of her husband's movements that he was home before 11:00 p.m. During further conversations with Mrs Kelly she explained that two days after the murder her husband told her to expect the police to come and interrogate him. She was asked why he had said that. He replied that he had been questioned before at a case of attempted murder on the island. He also informed his wife what she should do if anything should happen to him. Kelly also told his wife that he would rather commit suicide than serve another term of imprisonment. Soon after the conversations with his wife, Kelly did commit suicide.

When the police first interviewed Mrs Kelly they took possession of several items of the clothing Kelly had worn on 31 May, including a pair of plimsoles. She admitted that she had washed his shirt and a pair of jeans. Forensic science compared the footwear with the impression found in the spilled cement at the scene of the murder and found them identical. No two shoes bearing damage, marks and striations are identical to another, and in this case proved conclusively that Kelly was the murderer of Janice McCallum.

Mrs Kelly, after attending the inquest on her husband's death, called at the police station and made a third statement retracting the previous two, and said that when interviewed on previous occasions that she had taken some fortifying pills. She would not explain what these were but it was suspected that on the third occasion she had done likewise.

It was then necessary to prepare a file of evidence to present to the Isle of Man coroner to show that Michael Kelly had killed Janice McCallum. A hearing similar to a court case was held before the coroner with an all-male jury. The jury retired and returned a verdict that Kelly had killed Janice McCallum.

The system in the Isle of Man was that on reaching the verdict, the jury should return from their deliberations to the court room and, in the presence of everyone present, sign a document agreeing with the verdict. There was only one abstainer. It is not always easy to prove that a dead man committed murder.

Another case of a sexual predator satisfying his own desires on a perfectly innocent young holiday maker, causing much distress to both families involved.

# TWELVE

# Murder of Alan Livesey
## Bamber Bridge, 22 February 1979

THE MURDER OF ALAN LIVESEY, 14 years old, of Bamber Bridge, Lancashire, was a particularly heinous crime committed in unbelievable circumstances by his mother. It attracted wide publicity nationally through the press and media. After her conviction, several organisations endeavoured to prove her innocence.

As deputy head of CID on 22 February 1979, I was informed that the body of Alan Livesey had been found at his home. He was grotesquely bound and had been stabbed to death. According to normal practice I summoned the usual specialists, pathologist, forensic, fingerprint officers, and photographers. The scene was secured and the body removed for a post mortem to be conducted. In the morning I informed the assistant chief constable of the circumstances and, in view of the absence of the head of CID, I was appointed investigating officer. A murder control was set up at Bamber Bridge Police Station; little did I believe at that stage that the case would create such controversy as to the guilt of an offender.

When Alan Livesey was found he was wearing an army cadet uniform. He was bound and had been stabbed several times. A sock had been placed over his neck and he had been stabbed through it. Other wounds to the body had contributed to the cause of the death.

The circumstances leading up to his death were that in accordance with normal practice, his mother left Alan at home whilst she visited a nearby public house to have a few drinks with friends, without her husband, who was a night-shift worker. Alan was going through a typical growing youth's activities which lead him into conflict with the local police, much to the disapproval of his mother. On the night in question she remonstrated with him not to leave the house or get into any trouble.

When the body was found Margaret Livesey was interviewed at length and made a statement in which she explained that having had a few drinks with her friends, she was dropped off by car by a male friend near her home, she decided not to go home immediately but called on a neighbour where she was invited in for a further drink. Whilst at the neighbour's house she asked their son and another friend to go to her house and make sure Alan was alright. The two boys went to the Liveseys' home and checked both the front and the back door but found them both locked. They also knocked on the window but got no answer. They returned home and informed Mrs Livesey, who then gave them a key and asked them to go again and check on Alan. They entered the premises

*Alan Livesey, aged 14 years. Stabbed to death by his mother, Margaret Livesey*

and immediately smelt gas, the fire was not lit. They saw Alan lying on the floor. One of the boys moved Alan and attempted to apply mouth to mouth resuscitation, resulting in blood spurting out of a cut in his neck. The boys immediately ran home and told Mrs Livesey who at once entered her home, knelt down and held Alan in her arms. One of the boys ran and informed the police. When Mrs Livesey left home Alan was not wearing his army cadet uniform.

Enquiries were commenced in the immediate area. At that early stage I formed the impression that the answer lay in the neighbourhood. A press conference was held after which Margaret Livesey made an impassioned plea for the general public to help the police find the killer of her son. I was amazed at her demeanour and the lack of distress she displayed to the press and media.

The press in this type of case can be of considerable value, flooding the area with reporters to compose a story, and they sometimes discover information of value to the inquiry. That is why proper relationships are necessary between them and the police, an understanding of one another's role.

House to house enquiries began. When interviewed the next door neighbours gave vague information about noises coming from the Liveseys' house, but in little detail to be of much value. A press reporter informed me that the neighbours knew much more about the crime than that outlined in their statements. I arranged for them to be interviewed in depth.

Two days into the inquiry, still convinced that the answer to who committed the murder lay locally, I examined the blood-stained coat which Margaret Livesey had worn on 22 February. When Livesey cradled her dead son, on apparently seeing the body for the first time, she was bound to have blood smears on different parts of her clothing. These were obvious. But on a closer look at the sleeves of her coat I became aware of a spray type of blood effect; these can only be formed through an arm movement such as a striking motion. I have worked for many years with forensic scientists and on many occasions the geography of blood staining has been discussed. When an attack similar to that on Alan Livesey has taken place, sometimes very little blood will be apparent. However, when the body has been lying for some time, blood seepage will take place. But, after a striking motion, the blood will become more obvious in the form of 'splash and spray' effect. I am no expert in this field but in the light of experience and the aforementioned discussions I can, like anyone else, form an impression and an opinion. I now suspected Margaret Livesey had murdered her own son. I contacted the forensic scientist who was dealing with the case to arrange a meeting at Bamber Bridge Police Station. He was on a day off but he considered it of such importance that he agreed to meet me. I confided in him as to my observations and he agreed that the spray effect could have been caused by a striking motion in an attack. He then removed the coat for further examination. I did not divulge this information to anyone else in the murder squad until further tests were carried out on the garment.

The re-interview of the Liveseys' neighbours revealed a vastly different view of the incidents on the night of the murder. Although unaware of it, they actually heard the murder being committed. They recognised both Alan's and his mother's voices raised in a severe argument. One of them actually heard Alan call for help. They explained, understandably, that they did not want to get involved, but revealed that there was a long history of suspected abuse of Alan Livesey by his mother.

I briefed two extremely experienced detectives, Inspector Marriner and Detective Sergeant Biscombe, regarding the blood evidence and the information learned from the next door neighbours. I did not inform any other members of the squad regarding my findings or the present course of action. I arranged for Mrs Livesey to be brought to Bamber Bridge Police Station, to be interviewed by the two detectives under secure conditions. At the same time

I arranged for her husband to be interviewed at another police station. Margaret Livesey duly admitted that she had lost control of herself on returning from the public house. She had found Alan wearing his army cadet uniform and assumed that he had left the house in her absence, against her instructions, and in a blind rage stabbed him to death. She then arranged the scene to give the impression that someone else had committed the crime. On leaving the house she turned on the gas supply for some unknown reason. She then left the house and went to her neighbours for a drink. It was only on her admission that the murder weapon was established. When the house was being examined the murder weapon had not been found. As a precaution all possible sources for the weapon were explored. A cutlery drawer and its contents were removed from the kitchen and sent to the forensic laboratory as a precaution. Margaret Livesey admitted that she used a vegetable knife with a rivet missing from the handle, which she had cleaned and replaced back in the drawer. I telephoned the forensic laboratory with this information, resulting in the knife being recovered from the drawer.

Mrs Livesey's husband was allowed to see her at Bamber Bridge Police Station where she embraced him and admitted to him that she had murdered their son, Alan. She also admitted to other members of the family that she was responsible for Alan's death. At a later date, in the presence of a police woman, she admitted to her solicitor that she was responsible. Every statement taken during the inquiry for the first time was submitted to the Director of Public Prosecutions.

She appeared on trial at Preston Crown Court on two occasions, the first had to be abandoned owing to a juror problem. At the second, after a thorough trail, she was found guilty and sentenced to life imprisonment. Soon after the trial rumours were circulating of a miscarriage of justice.

Some years after the trial several individuals and organisations took up the case to seek to establish that

Margaret Livesey.
Convicted of
murdering her own
son and sentenced
to life imprisonment,
1979

Margaret Livesey had been the subject of a miscarriage of justice. The organisations included the group 'Justice' and the TV programme 'Rough Justice'. The individuals included the M.P. Stan Thorne and the journalist/broadcaster Ludovic Kennedy. Between them they spoke of new evidence, inaccuracies in the police evidence and alleged malpractice. In two of its shows the 'Rough Justice' programme declared sensational new details, indicating that Margaret Livesey was in prison for a crime that she did not commit. The producer and presenter of these programmes were severely criticised by the Lord Chief Justice for a deliberate attack on the integrity and reliability of the system of criminal justice.

Member of Parliament, Stan Thorne, brought up the case of Margaret Livesey in parliament in an attempt to gain a royal pardon, or at the very least a court appeal. The item was fully recorded in Hansard's parliamentary records, with a detailed response from the under-secretary of state, home department. Reference was made of the 'Rough Justice' programmes, and of representations made by Tom Sergeant from the organisation 'Justice', to the effect that Margaret Livesey was innocent.

However, a decision was made by the Home Secretary that the whole case should be reinvestigated by an officer of a superior rank to me from another police force. This was duly carried out by an assistant chief constable from Yorkshire, to my complete exoneration. It came to my attention that the only vital piece of information that came to light which would have been crucial at the time of my investigation, was to the effect that when Margaret Livesey left her neighbour's house to view Alan's body allegedly for the first time, she left blood staining on a piece of furniture, the inference being that she had been in contact with her son Alan before she went into that house. The neighbour, on finding the blood, wiped it away assuming that it was part of her female cycle. Vital evidence had been destroyed and was now only of circumstantial value.

The culmination of the reinvestigation led to an appeal being heard at the Old Bailey in London before the Lord Chief Justice and two other eminent judges. The deputy chief constable refused to allow me to read the reinvestigation report or even to attend the Old Bailey to represent the force, for some completely unknown reason. I got the impression that I was on trial. At the completion of the appeal the Lord Chief Justice prepared a twenty six page judgement which concluded with, 'we have carefully considered all these matters and we are not of the view that this conviction was in any way unsafe'. Livesey's appeal was dismissed.

So, seven years of argument, allegations and suspicions of a miscarriage of justice had all been negated by the highest legal authority in the land. That my decision to arrest and charge Margaret Livesey with the murder of her son after a four day investigation was the correct course of action. The then chief constable of Lancashire went into print seeking an apology from the BBC's 'Rough Justice' team, declaring that cases should be tried by judge and jury and not by media. No apology was forthcoming. To some extent I can understand the apprehension in the various organisations in suspecting that it seemed totally unbelievable that a mother could murder her son in such a gruesome manner. The facts in this case resulted in great sorrow being experienced by the family. The only injustice committed was to Alan Livesey, and to no other.

THIRTEEN

# Murder of Maud Hogan
## Lancaster, 17 March 1979

ON SATURDAY 17 MARCH 1979, 89-year-old Maud Hogan, a widow, was found dead in bed in her bungalow at Morley Close, Lancaster, by a care warden. I was a detective superintendent, second in command of the county's CID at the time, and immediately set up a murder control at Lancaster Police Station. This inquiry highlighted the absolute necessity for the utmost care in the control of the murder scene, and the provision of accurate information by all who entered the premises before my arrival.

Maud Hogan was found dead in bed wearing night attire and covered by bed covers. She had been battered about the head. The contents of the furniture in the room had been emptied onto the bed covers. This was an example of a thorough search for valuables with complete disregard for the occupant of the bed. It was not known if this search was done before, or after, the fatal blows were struck. In any case it was apparent that because of her age and infirmity she would not have been able to defend herself. The scene displayed a high degree of callousness by either a drunken person, a 'druggie' or a young, irresponsible person. The curtains were drawn in the bedroom and the doors were locked. This was confirmed by the care warden who had to use her pass key to enter the premises through the front door, leaving the conclusion that either someone Mrs Hogan knew had entered the house or the assailant had a key.

I summoned sixty detectives to the murder control, sealed the house and arranged search teams. I visited the house again with the specialists: pathologists, fingerprint officers, photographers and scientists. In the living room I found two spent matches and a button which appeared to have come off a man's suit. There was no reason for Maud Hogan to require matches and none were found in the house. Lesson one: I realised that the pathologist was a pipe smoker and he admitted that he had lit his pipe and thrown the matches into the living room bin. He apologised most profusely. I do not need to point out the significance if an assailant had left matches. The button was identified as coming from a detective sergeant's jacket who had also visited the scene.

The inquiry got into full swing with considerable effect on Maud Hogan's friends and relatives who may have visited her around the night of the murder. Maud had last been seen alive at 4:30 p.m. on Friday 16 March at her home, and she was found dead at 9:40 a.m. the following day. Enquiries revealed that the occupants of the pensioners' bungalows on the estate where Maud Hogan lived had for some time been abused by gangs of youngsters causing disturbances – noise, doors being knocked on late at night – to the extent that neighbours were becoming terrified to go out at night. One pensioner stated that there had been disturbances for years. I was informed that one night she heard a noise at the back of her house and saw the outline of a man leaning his arm on the bathroom window, with another man nearby. She told Maud Hogan about this and advised her to keep her windows and doors closed at all times. Other pensioners made similar references to events such as someone knocking on doors as late as 4:00 a.m. in the morning. My views began to lean towards the assailant possibly being a younger member of the local community. I made appeals through the press for anyone who knew Maud

Hogan and had been in touch with her recently to come forward.

This appeal brought in little information but a local lady, equally as infirm as Maud, came forward and informed me that on the evening before the discovery of Mrs Hogan's body, because of the previous disturbances, she had decided to call on Maud with a reminder to secure her premises. She walked along a path at the rear of Maud's house and saw that her bedroom window was open. She could not give a precise time. She called to Maud but got no response and assumed that she was asleep. This was crucial information and I immediately revisited the house. Examinations were still being conducted and I inspected the bedroom window, which was still closed. I was shocked to find mud marks on the windowsill and on the curtains. There were also 'jemmy' marks on the window signifying that it had been forced open. This altered the whole complex of the inquiry; we were now dealing with a burglary. When the neighbour passed Maud Hogan's bedroom she was probably either dead or the assailants were inside the premises. This was obvious owing to Mrs Hogan's lack of response to her neighbour's call.

I interviewed the first police officer at the scene and a detective inspector who was not now involved in the inquiry. He admitted that on entering the premises he had closed the bedroom window. His explanation was not taken lightly. The time wasted on the possibility of legitimate access to Maud Hogan's home was of 'mind blowing' proportions.

The reaction of the murder team when I explained the circumstances was obvious. It is essential in any murder inquiry that briefings and debriefings are conducted daily and that the team are fully aware of the state of the investigation at all times. Detectives working on murder inquiries extend themselves considerably, working long hours and sometimes travelling long distances to the murder control. In the main they are individuals selected because they have proven ability and stamina. There is no doubt that the forced entry into Maud Hogan's house would have been found in due course, but knowledge of the true circumstances are important at the earliest opportunity in order to help determine the facts.

Enquiries now continued with renewed determination to track or eliminate active burglars. It is sometimes amazing to learn of the relationship that exists between detectives and villains. In 1966 I was a detective sergeant at Morecambe. One day whilst walking with a detective constable near Morecambe market, I saw a known offender whom I had dealt with before. It was obvious that he was carrying something under his jacket. We stopped him and discovered that he was carrying a woman's handbag. He tried to explain that it was his wife's and he was going to meet her. Instead he found himself in Morecambe police cells. I soon established that the handbag was not his wife's and that he had snatched it from a woman at Morecambe market. I knew that he was an active burglar so I examined his shoes. I knew that a burglary had been committed at a doctor's surgery and the perpetrator had left a distinct shoe mark on some laundry when reaching to disconnect a burglar alarm. The mark was identical to this man's shoe. He then admitted to several offences of burglary. Such was his demeanour that we had a good laugh about the handbag. Some years later he appeared before a judge in London. When sentenced, he was so annoyed at the judge's comments that he leapt out of the dock and assaulted the judge.

On the seventh day of the inquiry, whilst in the murder control room at Lancaster I received a personal phone call. It was from the individual I have made reference to about the stolen handbag. He indicated that he had read my appeal for information. I arranged to meet him and he named the people responsible for the murder. He assured me that his information was correct. He would not tell me why he was informing on his contemporaries, but I got the feeling it was either revenge or that even he didn't condone the murder of aged pensioners. It was apparent that he passed the information to me rather than to an officer he didn't know.

I acted on his information and two local youths were arrested, charged with the murder of Maud Hogan and duly convicted.

This was a despicable murder of an 89-year-old female pensioner in her own bed on a sheltered estate. It was estimated that £100 was stolen from the premises, but to resort to violence to possibly to increase their ill-gotten gains was totally inexcusable. Some murder inquiries are difficult and prolonged, and require stamina and enthusiasm in order to achieve a result. It is so important that the manpower involved is fully briefed and debriefed daily. Others, like this one, benefit from luck and being in the right place at the right time.

# FOURTEEN

# Murder of Christopher Martin Johnstone

## 6 October 1979:
## The 'Handless Corpse' Case

IN SEPTEMBER 1979 I WAS promoted to the rank of chief superintendent in charge of the territorial police division of Chorley. Previously I was a detective superintendent, second in command of Lancashire constabulary CID. One month after leaving the CID a report was received that a corpse had been found in a flooded quarry within my division. This was to lead to extensive enquiries in the UK and abroad, particularly in New Zealand. The corpse was later identified as Christopher Martin Johnstone, a native of New Zealand and an international drug smuggler.

Johnstone's drug activities first came to the notice of an investigative journalist employed by the *Auckland Star* newspaper in New Zealand. He was informed that Johnstone was engaged in the organised crime of drug smuggling and importation in a wide area including America, Australia and New Zealand. The newspaper organised a team of reporters to look into the syndicate's influence in that vile trade and, because of the extent of his operating areas, they gave him the code name of 'Mr Asia'.

*Christopher Martin Johnstone, international drug smuggler whose handless corpse was discovered in a flooded quarry, 1979.*

In 1978, after twelve months' team work, the newspaper published the investigation results. The wide publicity resulted in threats being made and a warning that the drug syndicate had access to guns and would not hesitate to use them, leaving the obvious conclusion that the drug syndicate was well developed and dangerous. The true extent of their criminal activities was yet to be discovered. Johnstone had made a million dollars smuggling drugs in a wide area by employing couriers to transport drugs, mainly in specially converted suitcases, distance and expense being of little concern. Johnson lived the high life, purchasing designer clothing, Jaguar cars, jewellery for himself and his girlfriends, and expensive travel by Concord; in effect a luxurious lifestyle – but it was the manner of his death that brought the realisation that this was no ordinary killing.

Great efforts had been made to prevent identification, stripping the body naked, removing the hands to eliminate fingerprints, destroying the teeth to prevent dental evidence and finally to prevent facial recognition. That appears to have been the intention, although these gruesome actions were only partially completed, probably by someone who was acting on instructions but lacked the mental courage to carry them out fully. One vital mistake was the failure to remove an identifiable necklace with a medallion inscribed in Chinese from his neck. Johnstone's murder had been well planned, part of which was to send his current girlfriend on holiday to Spain, to 'get her out of the way'. However, whilst on holiday she saw details of the murder in a newspaper and identified the necklace and medallion. The corpse was then identified as Johnstone.

*Eccleston Delph, the flooded quarry, where Johnstone's body was discovered.*

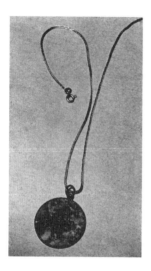

*The medallion by which Johnstone's girlfriend was able to identify him.*

In all horrendous murder inquiries of this sort background information is essential. In this case it meant making contact with the New Zealand police and Johnstone's history started to unravel. The extent of the investigation by the *Auckland Star* journalists also came to light along with police reports and the full realisation that Johnstone, referred to as 'Mr Big' or 'Mr Asia', was the leader of a drug smuggling organisation.

Martin Johnstone commenced work as a counter salesman in a menswear store in Auckland, but he was keen to make life more profitable. He initially turned to burglary and theft but moved on to the drug scene, his first conviction being for growing marijuana plants. Whilst working in Auckland, Johnstone met Andrew Maher, a Lancastrian from England. The two of them began to develop the marijuana drug trade with Maher and Johnstone reaping the profits. Their ambitions grew quickly into importing thai sticks (marijuana), a more profitable drug. They started to import using Dutch liners with direct access to Singapore, which on return to New Zealand cast drug-laden oil drums into the sea to be picked up later by inshore vessels. Business was beginning to boom. Johnstone was apparently not an extensively violent man, but with his financial power he may have paid others to carry out his instructions.

The whole scene changed dramatically when Johnstone and Maher met Terence John Clark, sometimes known as Sinclair, a native of Poverty Bay, Gisborne, New Zealand. Even during his school days Clark was regarded as 'a loner' with an unusual degree of violence. He wanted to display to his contemporaries that he was tough. It was thought that even in his school days he had carried a knife and he would use it. He moved to Auckland to seek employment but found himself in the hands of the police, committed a crime and was given a period in prison.

On release, whilst still on probation, he continued with his criminal activities, including receiving stolen property and expecting other offenders to do his dirty work. This was to become his common practice in the future. His criminal activities became more sophisticated when he turned to using explosives. In tight corners with the police, Clark became a police informer in an attempt to gain advantages for himself. Apart from being married, Clark had a girlfriend who was a heroin addict, and this was his first introduction into the drug world. He bought 24 capsules of heroin, but instead of giving them to his girlfriend he attempted to sell them, not knowing that an informant had turned the tables on him, and he was arrested by the police. The tablets turned out to be fake and he was released. He continued with his criminal activities and was duly arrested again for theft and the use of explosives. In 1971 he was sentenced to five years imprisonment. Whilst in prison Clark continued to display a devious and disruptive nature to fellow prisoners, whilst on the surface he gave the impression of a conformist. He met several prisoners who were of a similar disposition to himself. He even divorced his wife and remarried in the prison chapel, before being released from prison in 1974. His new wife was an alcoholic and heroin addict. His intention was to gain access to the more serious and more profitable world of drugs. His wife died a year later from an overdose of drugs.

Shortly, Clark again met Johnstone and Maher and formed a partnership which was to last for several years. They were entirely different characters and Johnstone may have thought he could use a hard man to carry out his criminal activities which he was incapable of doing himself. He misjudged Clark, not realising just how violent and vicious he was. Clark realised that vast sums of money could be made and must have gained more power in their organisation, to the detriment of Johnstone. Clark's temperament became apparent when a boat which he owned was raided by customs staff, and he was charged with the possession of drugs. He was convicted but later appealed and won. Clark was furious and came to the conclusion that someone had informed the authorities about him, so he set up a contract to have the alleged informer killed. There was a confrontation and the alleged informer left New Zealand for Australia. Clark's attitude became clouded from then on and he declared that anyone who was suspected of being an informer or disloyal and incapable of complying with the

*Andrew Maher*

syndicate's rules should be eliminated. This was ironic when bearing in mind that he had been a police informant himself.

Johnstone was by now very affluent and with his associates set up several companies in Singapore, probably to launder the money proceeds of drug dealings. The syndicate leaders, Johnstone and Clark, became more ambitious and through one of Johnstone's companies, purchased a sea-going yacht with the intention of importing vast amounts of drugs from Thailand. A great many problems ensued, resulting in the returns being far more limited than was planned, though considerable sums of money were realised.

Clark attempted importing of drugs on his own using his then girlfriend and her mother as couriers, sending them on a free holiday to Fiji to pick up two cartons of cigarettes and bring back to New Zealand. However it was later found that the cartons contained heroin. Clark suspected that his girlfriend had informed the police and he was arrested. Realizing that he was in a serious position and probably faced a long prison sentence,

Clark absconded and crossed over to Sydney, Australia. There he met some of his contemporaries who had been in prison with him, and soon discovered that there was a drugs market there. Clark also renewed his partnership with Johnstone on a visit to Singapore and continued to use couriers to carry on his supply line. Most of his staff were reliant on Clark to supply them with heroin and were themselves trapped in the vile trade as couriers and addicts. In the following years Clark tightened up his control of the drug syndicate to the detriment of Johnstone, Clark being a far stronger character than Johnstone. His organisation in Sydney was developing at a pace, in fact Clark's influence completely overshadowed the activities of Johnstone, who spent a great deal of his time in Singapore trying to develop other business interests, although his failing financial state became more obvious through his inability to pay bills, and his diminishing life style.

Clark maintained his syndicate power by corrupt payments to authorities and supplying practically unlimited funds and drugs to his couriers. He made it fairly plain that he would not tolerate disloyalty in any shape or form. It is apparent that some members of his syndicate were attracting the attention of the police and custom officials, some were arrested, and whilst in custody admissions were made. Clark, through his corruption of certain officials, found out about them. He was known to break out in violent rages and threatened revenge. Some of his couriers or members of the syndicate disappeared. Bodies were found with vital identification parts missing. It is very seldom that murders are committed in this way. Dismembered corpses are not uncommon in the UK, but it was quite apparent that Clark had developed his own gruesome techniques over a period of time and experience. He either committed the murder himself or paid others to follow his instructions. It takes a special type of criminal to adopt these methods.

Clark himself was duly arrested in Sydney for drug offences and suspicion of murder, but on it being discovered that he was wanted for drug offences in New Zealand, he was extradited there. A trial was held in New Zealand but once again he was found not guilty, a highly suspicious decision. Clark always said if you have the 'bread' (money) you can buy anything.

It came to his notice that enquiries in Australia were moving towards his arrest for murder, so a decision was made to move to the London to develop his trade in Europe and the United States. The pressure was certainly on in the Antipodes.

Clark's relationship with Johnstone, who was still mainly residing in Singapore, did not improve. Clark endeavoured to contact him with a view to establishing new markets in the Far East to supply his organisations in the UK. Eventually contact was made and Clark agreed to finance a drugs haul from Thailand to the sum of a quarter of a million dollars. Johnstone endeavoured to complete his transaction but was ripped off by Thailand traders, depriving Clark of the promised shipment and a large amount of money. This was the last straw for Clark who was furious and decided that Johnstone would have to be eliminated. He eventually convinced Johnstone to return to the UK on the pretext that he had a new deal for him in Scotland. Johnstone agreed, but knowing

*James Smith, Maher's accomplice in the murder of Johnstone*

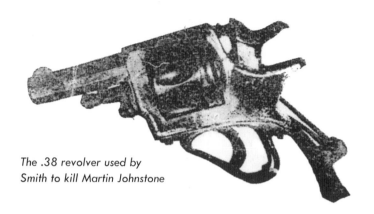

The .38 revolver used by
Smith to kill Martin Johnstone

Clark's background with syndicate defaulters, he must
have known that he was in great danger. Clark convinced
Maher to arrange to murder Johnstone, even though he
was a long standing friend.

Maher contacted a relative called James Smith in
Glasgow and recruited him to become a member of the
syndicate, but in particular to assist him to murder
Johnstone. Various items were bought to facilitate
the crime, the purchase of an axe, rope, a number of
weights including a lorry jack and a sheet of polythene.
It was obvious that Clark had given instructions on
how to disfigure the body and a disposal area had been
established. Clark had arranged for a gun to be sent by
courier from London to be delivered to Maher. Johnstone
flew to the UK on 7 October. Johnstone, Maher and Smith
set off from Leyland in Lancashire towards Glasgow,
allegedly to arrange a new drug deal in the North. After
travelling about thirty miles to Carnforth, just north
of Lancaster, Maher offered to let Johnstone drive the
vehicle. As Johnstone moved to change seats Maher shot
him twice in the head at point blank range. Maher then
drove the car back to a lock-up garage in Leyland where,
with Smith, they stripped the body, cut off the hands
and attempted to carry out further disfigurements. They
then drove the body to a flooded quarry, attached the

purchased weights and threw it into the water, failing to remove the only remaining identifiable piece of jewellery, the necklace and medallion. Smith was told to drive the vehicle used to kill Johnstone up to Scotland and dispose of it along with the severed hands and other items of property. This he failed to do according to instructions. If the necklace and medallion had been removed from Johnstone's neck it is doubtful if the body would ever have been identified. Similarly, with the removal of the hands and other disfigurements, it is unlikely there would have been a connection made with similar murders in Australia and New Zealand, as this was the first murder of its type committed in the UK.

Johnstone's body was found by amateur divers who thought that they had found a tailor's dummy, and information was passed to the police. The flooded quarry

*Halfpenny Lane leading to Eccleston Delph where Martin Johnstone's body was found (the 'Handless Corpse'), 1979*

*Police escorts transporting the prisoners to and from court during remand periods (between Chorley and Manchester), 1979*

was used by several organisations including the police for training purposes, and a Lancashire underwater search team recovered the body. A complete search of the quarry was carried out over several days and it was established that it was used as a dumping ground for stolen vehicles. One diver surfaced and pointed out that the last time he dived here he found a Jaguar car, but since then he now found that someone had gone down to the vehicle and removed the wheels. In addition he found the wheel brace used was still beside the vehicle.

Johnstone's girlfriend informed the police of his identity and where he had stayed. As a result the garage where the mutilation had taken place was discovered, revealing evidence of the event. Several samples of drugs, suitcases and other equipment were found. Maher and Smith were quickly arrested and soon afterwards Clark and several others were arrested in his luxury flat in London. In January 1981 twelve people were sent for trial at Lancaster Assize Court amid unprecedented security.

The trial took 115 days and cost more than £2 million. Nine defendants were sent to prison for various terms. Maher, Sinclair and Smith were all found guilty of murder and conspiracy to import and supply controlled drugs. All three were jailed for life with the recommendation that Sinclair and Maher serve a minimum of twenty years. In 1983 Maher was sectioned under the Mental Health Act in a secure hospital. Clark was sentenced to life imprisonment in top security Parkhurst prison on the Isle of Wight. He failed in an appeal and died in prison two years later aged 39 years. He must have found life very difficult in a UK prison, being deprived of his ability to pay his way out of any problem.

The true extent of Clark's murderous activities will never be known, but to develop his attempts to avoid identification by the means he used, one can only guess at it having taken several victims and probably years of experience to develop. In some circles it is estimated that Johnstone was his sixth victim. Such perverse activities in today's criminal calendar would be pointless with the development of DNA used to identify bodies or even body parts. The vast sums of money realised by Clark and Johnstone's syndicate will never be located.

Some years later a report published in a New Zealand newspaper referred to the drug scene in Clark and Johnstone's era compared to today's as being similar to 'tiddly winks'. I don't think so, but it indicates that there is always someone prepared to continue with this vile trade.

# FIFTEEN

# Retirement

**IN RETIREMENT LIFE IS A complete contrast
from stressful police work, to be taken at a much
slower pace.**

I retired from the Lancashire Constabulary in 1986, at
the age of fifty-five and in apparently good health, which
I resolved to keep that way. In other words it is a very
important stage of your life and planning is necessary on
future decisions, and without doubt health and fitness
are the most important. Whilst still a police officer
I was fortunate to have a modern police station with a
gymnasium on the top floor of the building which I used
daily for an hour before lunch, in addition I used to jog
for two or three nights per week at home. On retirement
I altered my exercise routine to walk between five to
eight miles three times a week, but currently I have
reduced the distance to two or three miles daily. It would
effortless to fall into the trap of taking it easy, resulting
in an expanding waistline.

The next problem is what to do with the rest of your
time. Despite a lack of training, I have made most of our
household furniture. Over the years my hobbies have
changed from the design of reproduction type furniture, to
wood turning and to stick making. I have made shepherds
crooks, hiking and thumb sticks using deer antlers, rams
horns, buffalo horns and wood. The use of ram and buffalo
horns are one of the most difficult to tackle, but over the
years I have had jigs and presses developed to make this
hobby slightly easier. I have won many awards at craft
shows but have never achieved what I call a top award;

*Turriff and District Pipe Band of which the author is an Honorary Vice President*

most of my exhibits go to such charities as the Royal British Legion where I have been a member in Scotland for fifty-five years.

My home town in Scotland also has a very progressive and much admired pipe band, with a variety of splendid uniforms and a first class membership.

The band holds an annual piping championship and at this occasion a chieftain is appointed for the event. For the past thirty-eight years his badge of office has been a stick bearing the names of the previous chieftains, the time had come for a replacement, which I designed. In 2011 I was invited to attend the championship and to present the stick to that year's chieftain, suitably dressed (wearing a kilt etc.), with one main difference that the stick would now be referred to as a 'crommack'. Prince Charles, on visiting Highland games some years ago, was presented with a beautiful ram's horn stick to which he restored the title of the 'Chieftain's Crommack'. I have recently been appointed an Honorary Vice President of the band, a position I take much pride in.

I have also been a member of Turriff and District Agricultural Association for sixty years, and in 2011 I received a presentation in recognition of that service. The main function of that association is to organise a summer show, an event second only to the Royal Highland Show in Scotland.

*The author, Clan Officer for the Hunter Clan in Scotland, holding one of his handmade Crommack sticks*

*Hunterston Castle, seat of the Hunter Clan, Ayrshire*

I am currently the Clan Officer for the Hunter Clan of Scotland. The clan meets at Hunterston Castle in Ayrshire. It is unique in that it was first built in the eleventh century and apart from some additions it is more or less in its original state. It has never been modernised as many other castles have and there are very few similar, if any, in Scotland. There are many Hunter Clan Associations throughout the world and each one has a Clan officer-in-charge. The clan in Scotland arranges an international gathering every three years to celebrate our history. The first Hunter arrived from Normandy and King David I of Scotland appointed him as the royal huntsman for the kings and queens of Scotland. A parchment signed by Robert II in 1374 confirmed ownership of the lands of Hunterston to the then chieftain. The castle is not occupied but is retained and preserved for prosperity.

Apart from age, retirement is a great thing. After twenty-five years I now consider myself as a consultant in that capacity. Make the most of it and look forward to the future, long may it last. Until I wrote this book I had nearly forgotten that I had been a police officer for thirty years. It was a phase in life that may have been strenuous at times, exciting and even rewarding, but is a period for reflection and should remain in the far distant past.

Murders and other heinous crimes make up a great deal of newspaper copy nowadays, but usually only the brief, sensational aspects are highlighted. My book gives more detail of the actual facts of a selection of cases, and shows how the killers were caught and convicted. We must never forget – and sometimes I think that the media does – that such appalling cases cause intense distress for everyone involved, from family right through to the police officers, and that the memories are never eradicated.